DO NOT REMOVE
CARDS FROM POCKET

1/29/97

ALLEN COUNTY PUBLIC LIBRARY
FORT WAYNE, INDIANA 46802

You may return this book to any agency, branch,

or bookmobile of the Allen County Public Library.

DEMCO

LEADERSHIP
INVESTING

LEADERSHIP INVESTING

Tapping into Your Business Knowledge & Experience to Create a Winning Investment Program

JOHN A. VANN

IRWIN
Professional Publishing®
Chicago • London • Singapore

Library of Congress Cataloging-in-Publication Data

Vann, John A.
    Leadership investing : tapping into your business knowledge & experience to create a winning investment program / John A. Vann.
        p.   cm.
    Includes index.
    ISBN 0-7863-0469-3
    1. Investments—United States.   2. Portfolio management.   3. Asset allocation.   I. Title.
    HG4910.V36   1997
    332.6—dc20   96–35440

Printed in the United States of America

1 2 3 4 5 6 7 8 9 0 DOC 3 2 1 0 9 8 7 6

INTRODUCTION

In the sea battles of World War I, German sailors were sometimes stranded in lifeboats for days or weeks after their ships had sunk. Ironically, the first men to die were the youngest. This phenomenon remained a mystery until it was realized that the older sailors, who had survived earlier sinkings, knew that the crisis could be weathered. Lacking such experience, the younger sailors perished because they saw themselves as trapped in a hopeless situation and fear overtook them. The moral? Become a seasoned sailor in the sea of investing, weathering the ups and downs of the market, and you'll come out a success.

There are scores of books on investing and understanding the stock market for the beginning investor—most of them helpful. A few of them good. The problem is most books simply cover the surface of investing by defining or explaining terms and products, or explaining how to buy stocks, open an IRA account, switch mutual funds, and so on.

IS THIS BOOK FOR YOU?

This book was written for the reader who is already familiar with investment basics and hungers to know more. This book covers advanced techniques, such as how to know when it is the best time in a business cycle to invest or pull back. It's about learning how to consistently beat the market, not just invest in it.

There's another way this book differs from books for beginners; it's not bogged down with pseudo-rules. Most basic investment books are written so that beginning investors can feel confident in following a set of rules. These pseudo-rules provide an easy template for the writer and help beginning investors feel they are in control of the investment process, but they're not. When I began as an investment professional, I was taught pseudo-rules by some of the very finest investment teachers in America. I never believed in these rules and never inflicted them on my clients. I realized early in my career, however, that there is a difference between pseudo-rules and effective principles. Pseudo-rules are sales tactics; effective principles are timeless strategies that work time and time again. I've since employed these investment principles successfully with my clients for over a quarter of a century.

WHO I AM AND WHY I'M A LEGEND IN THE INDUSTRY

Until recently, I was an investment consultant and financial advisor for a major national financial firm. I helped a wide variety of individuals, institutions, and corporations gain a clear understanding of their financial goals and develop a plan to accomplish them.

I live in Plano, Texas. Time and time again I've refused to move to New York—yet I've become a legend on Wall Street. How did I do it? I built up an asset base from scratch to more than $2 billion in less than 20 years. I did it my way, and now I'd like to share with you how I managed to succeed.

In August 1996, I opened my own registered investment advisory firm. All of my clients and all of my employees joined me in this new venture. To me, this is gratifying evidence of the soundness of my principles. It also, to me, is proof that if you put your clients' interests first—every day and with every transaction—your business will grow with their portfolio. This is the ultimate win-win situation for an advisor and his client.

In the 1970s, I realized that asset management was the most efficient way to build my investment business, so I concentrated on developing the tools to analyze asset managers, monitor performance, and conduct independent searches to locate the best and the brightest money managers in America.

My typical client is a corporation owned by an affluent first- or second-generation owner, who is either a sole owner or a majority owner. The corporation owners I represent are some of the wealthiest and most successful people in America.

Their corporations typically have a pension plan, a profit-sharing plan, a 401(k), and cash reserves. These clients typically control corporate accounts of $5 million to $100 million and individual assets between $1 million to $2 billion, depending on how they have liquidated or transferred the assets of their corporations. Often I start these relationships by providing professional services for one or all of a corporation's retirement plans, which often leads to providing the same services to the owners as individuals.

WHAT CAN YOU EXPECT FROM THIS BOOK?

What you will learn in this book are the same strategies I've used with the wealthiest and most successful men and women in the United States. But I need to warn you—this book is not written for the passive investor. That's the other guy's book. I have tried to work with the passive type of personality. I have given it my best shot. It is just a fact of life that the passive personality type will most likely amble to the bank and buy Treasury bills. There is nothing wrong with that, but no one is going to achieve a dignified retirement by owning T-bills.

Decision makers are, by nature, "type A" personalities (impatient, single-minded, driven, tireless individuals who take pride in getting more than the job done, not just show-ing up each day. He or she is probably a workaholic who has hardly seen the family in weeks.

I have written this book for *you,* Mr. or Ms. over-responsible, all-or-none, crisis-addicted decision maker. I would rather have you balk for a moment at my description, but then learn to use your traits and skills to your advantage to make correct investment decisions, than flatter you and allow you to go on to make disastrous investment decisions.

This book will teach you how to beat the stock market by a factor of two, and I will give you portfolios that do this utiliz-ing tools I developed. Famous entrepreneurs like Ross Perot, Harold Simmons, and Warren Buffett became rich because they knew how to use these tools. I will provide you with the closest thing to a crystal ball for understanding what lies ahead and how your investments will react to future events.

As you study these pages, you will understand why stocks and, yes, bonds are the investments of choice for successful entrepreneurs.

Here's a question I'd like to pose to you: Why do most investors do poorly when it comes time to buy or sell? Answer: The average investor tends to be attracted to funds that show recent spectacular growth. But by the time the investor enters that mutual fund, the growth spurt has cooled. The expected high gains fail to appear, and the investor loses patience and sells, locking in a loss.

The irony is that growth investments' inherent volatility alternately spooks and attracts investors. The typical "investor" tends to buy at the end of a growth cycle and then sell prematurely. This can cause the investor to lose money in equities, an investment that historically pays off for entrepreneurs. I see individuals every day who excel in their professions—engineers, doctors, lawyers—who are functionally illiterate when it comes to making investment management decisions. They invest their money in vehicles that barely keep up with inflation, and overload on new "hot" deals. They don't really understand what drives the economy or themselves, or how to make an investment decision.

These intelligent, effective decision makers often make bad investment decisions **because the very attributes that make them effective decision makers—direction, focus, and fast reaction—work against them as investors.** In their chosen professions, they would never blindly believe what the salesman says. They would never react before understanding all the facts.

In the 1970s, when every Wall Street firm in town was selling oil and gas limited partnerships, why weren't professional oil men investing in these areas? Because they understood the oil business and knew it was impossible for the public investor to make money in the structure of an oil limited partnership. These guys weren't stupid: Many became general partners in these limited partnerships. They were getting a percentage of the money before any money went into drilling for oil. The smart oil guys were falling on the ground laughing at "Wall Street" playing "oil men" and "wildcats."

HOW DO YOU DEFEND YOURSELF?

You learn to think like an entrepreneur.

The best thing a legitimate financial advisor can do for you, aside from calling out a warning, is to inspire you to think about investing in the same way you think about your business.

THE SELF-MANAGED INVESTOR

Here is a common scenario. Today's typical self-managed investor has been "sold" a portfolio of randomly scattered assets. He has received a variety of sales prompts from friends, advertisements, bankers, the media, and his stock-broker. Each investment seems like a great singular transaction idea at the time, but the entire portfolio is not balanced nor even considered as a whole. What I see walk in my door, in most cases, is a self-managed investor with a portfolio that makes no sense, has random assets with high fees or back-end commission traps—and the investor has often been sold these goods at the peak of a market/asset cycle.

FIRST TIP

Did you know that most people—and in fact, most professionals—who invest in the stock market come nowhere close to even matching the index returns? (An index is the average return of all the stocks, e.g., the Dow Jones 30 Industrials or the Standard and Poor's 500.) In other words, applied theories do not beat the standard market average. In fact, 70 percent of all mutual funds perform lower than their respective indexes. In most cases, I can increase self-managed investors' returns by advising them to buy pure index funds. By so doing, they also avoid the high fees of mutual funds, but give up an 800 number to call at 3 A.M. and forfeit the four-color brochures. Would you prefer splash or profit?

SECOND TIP

Trying to time the market doesn't work either. Peter Lynch, former portfolio manager of The Magellan Fund from Fidelity, pointed out that more than half the shareholders in this fund lost money, based on when they bought and sold their shares. Magellan had delivered investment performance of more than 18 percent a year for the last 10 years, as of December 1995, and more than 22 percent a year since inception in 1963.

Martin Zweig, a well-known investment manager recently retained by Morningstar (the mutual fund research organization) to track cash flows in and out of the nation's leading growth funds, discovered similar results in other mutual funds.

As shown in Exhibit 1, the contrast of returns of the investments themselves as compared to the returns of investors was startling: A group of 219 growth mutual funds had an annual average compound return of +12.5 percent for the

EXHIBIT 1

The Disparity between Investment Returns and Investor's Returns

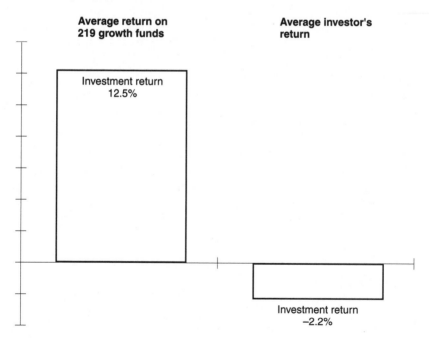

five years ending in June 1994. But the individual investors lost 2.2 percent a year with this same group of growth funds. Why? Because they tried to time the market and ended up getting burned by getting in or out of the market at the wrong time.

THE POINT IS—THIS DOESN'T HAVE TO HAPPEN TO YOU!

Let's jump right in and get started. The premise of this book is: *How to double the stock market over a market cycle.* (Note: I did not say you could double your returns every day, hour, or year, but every market cycle.) You'll learn how to do this by gaining an understanding of the ins and outs of investments and markets following a proven investment strategy, and by staying on course.

That's it. Once you have this map, you'll have the tools to craft an investment portfolio that will outperform 90 percent of investors.

C O N T E N T S

PART ONE

BECOME AN EXPERT
ON THE MARKET

1
CHAPTER

How to Double the Stock Market—A Quick Start

Before we go any further, I'd like to "prime the pump," so to speak—giving you 10 basic truths that act as a foundation for the entire process. Understanding and using these points will take you a long way in doubling the stock market.

Truth #1: *Become grounded. There IS risk.* Make it your friend not your enemy. John and Mary Q. Public want investing to be easy and without risk—that is impossible. Yet not only do they want it, they expect it. You've got to understand, "What's so risky about investing—is risk."

Truth #2: *Nothing on Wall Street is gained without a toll.* No-load mutual funds are NOT free! Too few people have read a prospectus. (Pick up any prospectus, they are all pretty much the same, and read "fees and expenses.") Total fund operating expenses can range from 1.0 to 2.48 percent per annum. And yes, even no-load mutual funds pay brokerage commissions when they buy stocks or bonds for their portfolios. This is rarely adequately disclosed to shareholders, however.

Still, a revolution has just taken place in the investment industry, and many mutual funds are now willing to waive all loads, up-front commissions, and all deferred sales charges.

Truth #3: *Many mutual funds invest in "derivatives" that can dramatically deplete capital in a short time.* Derivatives are a form of investment created by combining parts of different securities, and they are considered by many in the investment world to be highly speculative. Institutional and conservative investors avoid them due to their risky nature.

Truth #4: *Often the stock brokers from major, respected firms are paid more for pushing a particular product.* Special incentives are also paid to no-load mutual fund phone "service representatives" to steer clients into alternative funds— funds that have not done well and need more money.

Truth #5: *A majority of investors overreact to headlines generated by journalists' deadlines and abandon their long-term plans out of fear and greed.* This is one of the most destructive practices an investor can do to his investment program.

Truth #6: *The central bank (federal reserve) wants to maintain the Equilibrium:*
Equilibrium =

- Inflation at 4 percent
- Gross Domestic Product at 4 percent
- Money Supply at 4 percent
- Interest Rates at 4 percent

We will discuss in Chapter 2 how knowing this fundamental principle (4 – 4 – 4 – 4) can help you evaluate the economy so that you can position yourself to take advantage of the upcoming stage in the business cycle.

Truth #7: *News and politics DO NOT impact the market!* While the market may seem to be reacting to news items, it is a temporary reflection of investor reaction; the fundamental condition of the market is not really affected.

People use the news as an excuse not to invest. You must stay invested. Being out just a few days in a decade can dramatically impact your results.

Truth #8: *You must invest in stocks and keep a substantial portion of your assets in stocks.*

Truth #9: *Like the toss of a coin, what happened last month, quarter, or year has no real meaningful impact on the future.* What *does* affect your investment results is the business cycle. You need to know what constitutes an entire cycle and where we are in the cycle at any given time to be able to take advantage of the opportunities each phase offers.

Truth #10: *Know, understand, and avoid the four great lies in investment advertising:* the Selected Time Period Lie, the Account Selectivity Lie, the Account Attrition Lie, and the Replacement Lie.

- *Selected Time Period Lie*—Have you ever noticed how in many mutual fund ads you see where the line chart looks spectacular? This is because any mutual fund can pick any time series to measure themselves. Read the fine print. What it says is that this fund has the number one record for 16.14 months in the left-handed giraffe market.
- *Account Selectivity Lie*—An investment manager can select an account on which to show performance. It

might be the oldest account, the largest account, the smallest account—but rest assured, it is one of the better performing accounts that gets the spotlight.

- *Account Attrition Lie*—Any investment manager or mutual fund loses clients each year. The rate has historically been about 10 percent. Presumably, these are not the best performing clients. Over a five-year period, if an investment manager presents a record stating, "Over the past five years my clients have received an *x* percent rate of return," they are only really looking at the top 50 percent who are left after attrition.

- *Replacement Lie*—Yes, it's true. If I have Mutual Fund A and I hire Peter Lynch, and if Peter Lynch can prove that he made more than 51 percent of the decisions in Fidelity Magellen, I can advertise his track record as if it were my own.

P.S. Ever wonder why mutual fund families use so many mutual funds? So the chance of being high in something increases.

Although not all of these truths will be specifically addressed, they will become evident as we move through the book. Now that you know my 10 truths, you're ready to put them into action and become your own expert. First step? Know the market.

2
CHAPTER

Why You Need to Become Your Own Expert

My father was a military officer who had risen to a leadership position during the Vietnam War. I remember when I was 13 years old, watching my father get ready for the most important meeting of his life. He was to address the Joint Chiefs of Staff at the Pentagon. He prepared for his speech relentlessly. On the day of his speech, his clothes were impeccably pressed and his boots highly shined. He knew the impact his speech would have; it could possibly change the course of the Vietnam War. But that night, he came home mad as hell, so mad he could hardly talk. His speech had been canceled; he had been denied access to the Joint Chiefs. The reason was not earthshaking. They simply did not want to hear the truth because it contradicted their "conventional wisdom."

THE REAL "TRUTH" BEHIND "CONVENTIONAL WISDOM"

So what does this have to do with investing and decision making today? Truth does not sell stocks or mutual funds. It is "success" story ads at the back of magazines that sell mutual funds. Truth has little to do with it. Fear and greed replace facts!

Let's take the point a little further. When I entered the investment business, I wanted to be successful. I quickly figured out that I would either have to work with a great number of small individuals at kitchen tables, or seek out the very wealthy and provide a valuable service to them. The first thing I did was identify two highly visible groups of wealthy investors. The first consisted of those families owning the most successful business in every major U.S. city. The second most visible category of investors was banks. I then tried to figure out what I could do to provide value-added service to these two groups. I called several wealthy individuals and was told that their assets were being managed by bank trust departments. I asked each the logical question, "How are you doing?"

> I called several wealthy individuals and was told that their assets were being managed by bank trust departments. I asked each the logical question, "How are you doing?"
>
> Most replied, "I don't know."

Most replied, "I don't know."

Then I went to the banks. I asked what services I could provide to these institutions. They said, "You can't provide any!"

Out of frustration, I said to the head of a local trust department, "Nobody seems to know how you're doing. Don't you want to show your clients that you are achieving their objectives?"

His answer was, "No! Why would we want our clients to know how we are doing? If they had a way to measure us, they might terminate the relationship. No thank you."

That was when it hit me. Bureaucratic consciousness! Bureaucracies do things the way they have always been done—without questioning, self-examination, or concern for setting standards of accountability and responsibility. The gatekeepers to the Pentagon told my father he could not enter; the banks told me I could not enter, either.

I was angry and frustrated; this motivated me to gather independent data and measure the performance of bank trust departments around the country. And you know what I found, right?

Bank trust departments' performances were appalling. In fact, at that time their performance was so dismal that the banks' own CDs were averaging better than their trust department investment portfolios! Banks, like the Pentagon and the 90 Wall Street retail firms, coveted control and ownership but shunned accountability. I found no difference between the morality of the Joint Chiefs and the heads of bank trust departments. With a vengeance that my father must also have felt, I launched an entire industry of investment consulting by linking investment responsibility to accountability. Until then, it had never been done.

That provided tremendous satisfaction. I have always felt my job was not so much about making investment decisions as providing people a level playing field, the truth and, therefore, accountability. Only when you have the truth can you make an objective and informed decision (it's that simple). **To win— become an informed investor.**

Some people shun the truth. It creates discomfort. They get angry and leave. I let them. As a result of my attitude and quest for a level playing field and investment truth, my client base today is made up of some of the nation's—in fact, the world's—wealthiest and smartest investors. Effective decision makers want accountability, accept responsibility, and are willing to make appropriate changes when necessary. This chapter is about becoming your own expert. I didn't say investment advisor; I said expert. An expert is defined as a person with a high degree of skill in or knowledge of a certain subject. That's what you are about to get. So we will start by understanding how the investment markets work and the macro-economic variables that affect your investments.

UNDERSTANDING THE BASICS OF MARKET PERFORMANCE

Like any good entrepreneur, an entrepreneurial investor must have a clear understanding of what his options are. You can't make a sound business decision unless you see the whole picture. In the same way, an investor has to have a broad perspective of the market in order to make the right investment decisions and to see opportunities that others may miss.

Exhibit 2–1 provides an overview of the total return performance of large company stocks ("large capitalized equities") throughout the past 70 years. Each year since 1926 is listed in tabular format. The performance of large company stocks is listed for each year. A summary of observations is alongside of the tables. For example in 1926 large stocks were up 11.6 percent. In 1934 large stocks were down –1.4% for the one-year period.

EXHIBIT 2–1

Large Company Stocks—Total Return (1926–1995)

Calendar Year Total Return

Year	Return	Year	Return	Year	Return
1926	11.6%	1950	31.7%	1974	-26.5%
1927	37.5%	1951	24.0%	1975	37.2%
1928	43.6%	1952	18.4%	1976	23.8%
1929	-8.4%	1953	-1.0%	1977	-7.2%
1930	-24.9%	1954	52.6%	1978	6.6%
1931	-43.3%	1955	31.6%	1979	18.4%
1932	-8.2%	1956	6.6%	1980	32.4%
1933	54.0%	1957	-10.8%	1981	-4.9%
1934	-1.4%	1958	43.4%	1982	21.4%
1935	47.7%	1959	12.0%	1983	22.5%
1936	33.9%	1960	0.5%	1984	6.3%
1937	-35.0%	1961	26.9%	1985	32.2%
1938	31.1%	1962	-8.7%	1986	18.5%
1939	-0.4%	1963	22.8%	1987	5.2%
1940	-9.8%	1964	16.5%	1988	16.8%
1941	-11.6%	1965	12.5%	1989	31.5%
1942	-20.3%	1966	-10.1%	1990	-3.2%
1943	25.9%	1967	24.0%	1991	30.5%
1944	19.8%	1968	11.1%	1992	7.7%
1945	36.4%	1969	-8.5%	1993	10.0%
1946	-8.1%	1970	4.0%	1994	1.3%
1947	5.7%	1971	14.3%	1995	37.4%
1948	5.5%	1972	19.0%		
1949	18.8%	1973	-14.7%		

☐ = Loss Year

# of Years = 70

# of Loss Years = 21, or 30%

Avg. *Loss* per Year = 12.7%

Longest Consecutive Years with a *Loss* = 4 (twice) (1929–1932 and 1939–1942)

The Annualized Return for the Following 4 Years after That 4-Year Loss = 31.6% and 17.3%

Source: *SBBI 1996 Yearbook.* Chicago: Ibbotson Associates, 1996. Reprinted with permission.

11

As you examine this table, you'll notice that there are very few periods when you would have earned a negative total return. So, why are so many investors afraid of the stock market? One reason is that when the market is experiencing a significant down trend, it tends to occur for a period lasting a year or more. Though this situation holds obvious challenges, it provides savvy investors with potentially attractive opportunities, as well.

Investment managers know that many individual investors bail out at the bottom! Entrepreneurs buy when others are selling, and this is also a basic principle of investing. Looking at the whole scheme of things, we see that it is difficult to find any longer-term period where the large cap market compounded at a rate under 10 percent a year.

If you study Exhibit 2–2 and follow the first row from 1926 to 1995, you observe that the market returned an average of 10.5 percent per year. Even if you were an unlucky soul who invested all your money prior to the great crash of October 1929, you still would have averaged 9.7 percent per year had you stayed the course and held your portfolio until 1995. Bear in mind that this performance level would have been achieved even though the market declined four years in a row after you started.

What does this say about equity investments? There really are not that many down years—and many more up years. And over the long term, large cap stocks tend to grow at about 10 percent a year. Understanding these facts is one of the basic principles of successful long-term investing.

What does this mean for other asset classes? Let's take a look at the long-term government bond market.

As you see in Exhibit 2–3, bonds have earned 5.2 percent over the long term. Generally bonds have averaged about

EXHIBIT 2 – 2

Large Company Stocks
Total Annualized Return for Period Ending 1995

Time Period	Return	Time Period	Return	Time Period	Return
1926–1995	10.5%	1950–1995	12.6%	1974–1995	13.2%
1927–1995	10.5%	1951–1995	12.2%	1975–1995	15.6%
1928–1995	10.2%	1952–1995	11.9%	1976–1995	14.6%
1929–1995	9.7%	1953–1995	11.8%	1977–1995	14.1%
1930–1995	10.0%	1954–1995	12.1%	1978–1995	15.4%
1931–1995	10.7%	1955–1995	11.2%	1979–1995	16.0%
1932–1995	11.9%	1956–1995	10.8%	1980–1995	15.8%
1933–1995	12.2%	1957–1995	10.9%	1981–1995	14.8%
1934–1995	11.6%	1958–1995	11.5%	1982–1995	16.4%
1935–1995	11.9%	1959–1995	10.8%	1983–1995	16.0%
1936–1995	11.3%	1960–1995	10.7%	1984–1995	15.4%
1937–1995	11.0%	1961–1995	11.0%	1985–1995	16.3%
1938–1995	12.0%	1962–1995	10.6%	1986–1995	14.8%
1939–1995	11.7%	1963–1995	11.3%	1987–1995	14.4%
1940–1995	11.9%	1964–1995	10.9%	1988–1995	15.7%
1941–1995	12.4%	1965–1995	10.7%	1989–1995	15.5%
1942–1995	12.9%	1966–1995	10.7%	1990–1995	13.0%
1943–1995	12.7%	1967–1995	11.5%	1991–1995	16.6%
1944–1995	12.5%	1968–1995	11.1%	1992–1995	13.3%
1945–1995	12.4%	1969–1995	11.1%	1993–1995	15.3%
1946–1995	11.9%	1970–1995	11.9%	1994–1995	18.0%
1947–1995	12.4%	1971–1995	12.2%	1995–1995	37.4%
1948–1995	12.5%	1972–1995	12.1%		
1949–1995	12.7%	1973–1995	11.8%		

Unlucky Soul

Mr. Unlucky Soul invested $100 in the stock market January 1, 1929.

Starting Market Value	=	$100
His First Year,	1929 = –8.4%	$91.6
His Second Year,	1930 = –24.9%	$68.8
His Third Year,	1931 = –43.3%	$39.0
His Fourth Year,	1932 = –8.2%	$35.8
Ending Market Value	=	$35.8
Annualized Return 4 Years	= –22.6%	

Lucky Soul

Mr. Unlucky Soul stayed in the stock market. As of December 31, 1995

Ending Market Value	=	$33,537.5
Annualized Return 70 Years =	9.7%	

Source: *SBBI 1996 Yearbook*. Chicago: Ibbotson Associates, 1996. Reprinted with permission.

13

EXHIBIT 2-3

Long-Term Government Bonds
Total Annualized Return for Period Ending 1995

Time Period	Return	Time Period	Return	Time Period	Return
1926–1995	5.2%	1950–1995	5.7%	1974–1995	10.1%
1927–1995	5.1%	1951–1995	5.8%	1975–1995	10.4%
1928–1995	5.1%	1952–1995	6.0%	1976–1995	10.4%
1929–1995	5.2%	1953–1995	6.1%	1977–1995	10.1%
1930–1995	5.2%	1954–1995	6.2%	1978–1995	10.8%
1931–1995	5.2%	1955–1995	6.2%	1979–1995	11.5%
1932–1995	5.4%	1956–1995	6.4%	1980–1995	12.4%
1933–1995	5.2%	1957–1995	6.7%	1981–1995	13.5%
1934–1995	5.3%	1958–1995	6.7%	1982–1995	14.4%
1935–1995	5.2%	1959–1995	7.1%	1983–1995	12.6%
1936–1995	5.2%	1960–1995	7.3%	1984–1995	13.7%
1937–1995	5.2%	1961–1995	7.1%	1985–1995	13.5%
1938–1995	5.3%	1962–1995	7.3%	1986–1995	11.9%
1939–1995	5.2%	1963–1995	7.3%	1987–1995	10.6%
1940–1995	5.2%	1964–1995	7.5%	1988–1995	12.4%
1941–1995	5.2%	1965–1995	7.7%	1989–1995	12.8%
1942–1995	5.3%	1966–1995	7.9%	1990–1995	11.9%
1943–1995	5.3%	1967–1995	8.1%	1991–1995	13.1%
1944–1995	5.4%	1968–1995	8.7%	1992–1995	11.6%
1945–1995	5.5%	1969–1995	9.1%	1993–1995	12.8%
1946–1995	5.3%	1970–1995	9.7%	1994–1995	10.2%
1947–1995	5.5%	1971–1995	9.6%	1995–1995	31.7%
1948–1995	5.6%	1972–1995	9.4%		
1949–1995	5.7%	1973–1995	9.6%		

Selected Periods Ending 1995		
From	**Stocks**	**Bonds**
1926	10.5%	5.2%
1941	12.4%	5.2%
1963	11.3%	7.3%
1969	11.1%	9.1%
1971	12.2%	9.6%
1973	11.8%	9.6%
1975	15.6%	10.4%
1991	16.6%	13.1%

Yes, the 1995 Rally really did produce a +31.7% year in Long-Term Government Bonds

Source: *SBBI 1996 Yearbook.* Chicago: Ibbotson Associates, 1996. Reprinted with permission.

half the rate of return of stocks. There are some exception years, as you will discover, but for planning purposes, consider 2:1 premium of stocks over bonds, and occasionally a 1.5:1 premium. There have been negative periods for the bond market and just like with stocks, they appear in clumps. (See Exhibit 2–4.) If you then compare the negative periods for both asset classes, you can see that these negative periods often happen at different times. (See Exhibit 2–5.)

Alas! Bond investors, like stock investors, usually sell their bonds after a few bad years and lock in losses. Exhibit 2–6 shows the lost profits.

After each down period of the market when investors pulled negative returns, there was a strong and sustained recovery period. This chart shows that after a six-month period of decline, the bond market was yielding solid returns 18 months later.

But what's the real lesson here? If an investor wants to improve his standard of living, he needs to own stock. If a person keeps his money in government bonds for the long term, his returns of about 5 percent annually will only keep him up with inflation. His money won't lose its buying power, but he's not getting additional buying power from his bond market returns.

What does the entrepreneur want? Is it really any different from what the average investor wants? Or does the entrepreneur just go about it differently? Before answering these questions, we need to take a closer look at the motivating forces behind inflation and the entire economy.

What other liquid investments are available? Treasury bills? What do Treasury bills return over the long term? Just a little over the underlying inflation rate (3.7 percent to be exact), and inflation averages 3.1 percent. (See Exhibit 2–7

EXHIBIT 2-4

Long-Term Government Bonds—Total Return (1926–1995)

Calendar Year Total Return

Year	Return	Year	Return	Year	Return
1926	7.8%	1950	0.1%	1974	4.4%
1927	8.9%	1951	-3.9%	1975	9.2%
1928	0.1%	1952	1.2%	1976	16.8%
1929	3.4%	1953	3.6%	1977	-0.7%
1930	4.7%	1954	7.2%	1978	-1.2%
1931	-5.3%	1955	-1.3%	1979	-1.2%
1932	16.8%	1956	-5.6%	1980	-3.9%
1933	-0.1%	1957	7.5%	1981	1.9%
1934	10.0%	1958	-6.1%	1982	40.4%
1935	5.0%	1959	-2.3%	1983	0.7%
1936	7.5%	1960	13.8%	1984	15.5%
1937	0.2%	1961	1.0%	1985	31.0%
1938	5.5%	1962	6.9%	1986	24.5%
1939	5.9%	1963	1.2%	1987	-2.7%
1940	6.1%	1964	3.5%	1988	9.7%
1941	0.9%	1965	0.7%	1989	18.1%
1942	3.2%	1966	3.7%	1990	6.2%
1943	2.1%	1967	-9.2%	1991	19.3%
1944	2.8%	1968	-0.3%	1992	8.1%
1945	10.7%	1969	-5.1%	1993	18.2%
1946	-0.1%	1970	12.1%	1994	-7.8%
1947	-2.6%	1971	13.2%	1995	31.7%
1948	3.4%	1972	5.7%		
1949	6.4%	1973	-1.1%		

☐ = Loss Year

# of Years = 70

# of Loss Years = 19, or 27%

Avg. *Loss* per Year = 3.2%

Longest Consecutive Years with a *Loss* = 4 (1977–1980)

The Annualized Return for the Following 4 Years after That 4-Year Loss = 13.6%

Source: *SBBI 1996 Yearbook.* Chicago: Ibbotson Associates, 1996. Reprinted with permission.

16

Large Company Stocks & Long Term Government Bonds
Total Return (1926–1995)

	Stocks	Bonds
1926		
1927		
1928		
1929	–8.4%	
1930	–24.9%	
1931	–43.3%	–5.3%
1932	–8.2%	
1933	–1.4%	–0.1%
1934	–1.4%	
1935		
1936		
1937	–35.0%	
1938		
1939	–0.4%	
1940	–9.8%	
1941	–11.6%	
1942	–20.3%	
1943		
1944		
1945		
1946	–8.1%	–0.1%
1947		–2.6%
1948		
1949		

Calendar Year Total Return

	Stocks	Bonds
1950		
1951		–3.9%
1952		
1953	–1.0%	
1954		
1955		–1.3%
1956		–5.6%
1957	–10.8%	
1958		–6.1%
1959		–2.3%
1960		
1961		
1962	–8.7%	
1963		
1964		
1965		
1966	–10.1%	
1967		–9.2%
1968		–0.3%
1969	–8.5%	–5.1%
1970		
1971		
1972		
1973	–14.7%	–1.1%

	Stocks	Bonds
1974	–26.5%	
1975		
1976		
1977	–7.2%	–0.7%
1978		–1.2%
1979		–1.2%
1980		–3.9%
1981	–4.9%	
1982		
1983		
1984		
1985		
1986		
1987		–2.7%
1988		
1989		
1990	–3.2%	
1991		
1992		
1993		
1994		–7.8%
1995		

= Loss Year

# of Years = 70

# of Loss Years for Both
Stocks & Bonds = 4, or 2.5%

Avg. *Loss per Year* = 9.8%

Source: *SBBI 1996 Yearbook*. Chicago: Ibbotson Associates, 1996. Reprinted with permission.

17

EXHIBIT 2-6

Market Returns—US Government Bonds
(Returns 18 months after the 6-month decline)

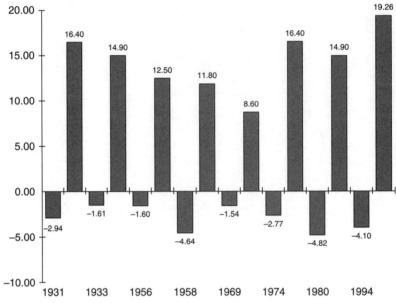

Source: *SBBI 1996 Yearbook.* Chicago: Ibbotson Associates, 1996. Reprinted with permission.

for the long-term averages of Treasury bills.) Exhibit 2–8 shows the year-by-year return of Treasury bills.

In the past 70 years, Treasury bills have averaged about 4 percent, government bonds about 5 percent, corporate bonds about 6 percent, and stocks about 10 percent (all rounded to the nearest percent). These are the basic asset classes that concern everyone in investing: stocks, government and corporate bonds, and Treasury bills.

The other component critical to investment success is the impact of inflation. Let's take a look at the rate of inflation through these same years. (See Exhibit 2–9 for the rate of inflation each year since 1926.)

US Treasury Bills
Total Annualized Return for Period Ending 1995

Time Period	Return	Time Period	Return	Time Period	Return
1926–1995	3.7%	1950–1995	5.2%	1974–1995	7.2%
1927–1995	3.7%	1951–1995	5.2%	1975–1995	7.2%
1928–1995	3.7%	1952–1995	5.3%	1976–1995	7.3%
1929–1995	3.7%	1953–1995	5.4%	1977–1995	7.4%
1930–1995	3.7%	1954–1995	5.5%	1978–1995	7.5%
1931–1995	3.7%	1955–1995	5.6%	1979–1995	7.5%
1932–1995	3.8%	1956–1995	5.7%	1980–1995	7.4%
1933–1995	3.8%	1957–1995	5.8%	1981–1995	7.1%
1934–1995	3.9%	1958–1995	5.9%	1982–1995	6.6%
1935–1995	3.9%	1959–1995	6.0%	1983–1995	6.3%
1936–1995	4.0%	1960–1995	6.1%	1984–1995	6.1%
1937–1995	4.1%	1961–1995	6.2%	1985–1995	5.7%
1938–1995	4.1%	1962–1995	6.3%	1986–1995	5.6%
1939–1995	4.2%	1963–1995	6.4%	1987–1995	5.5%
1940–1995	4.3%	1964–1995	6.5%	1988–1995	5.5%
1941–1995	4.4%	1965–1995	6.6%	1989–1995	5.4%
1942–1995	4.5%	1966–1995	6.7%	1990–1995	4.9%
1943–1995	4.5%	1967–1995	6.8%	1991–1995	4.3%
1944–1995	4.6%	1968–1995	6.9%	1992–1995	4.0%
1945–1995	4.7%	1969–1995	6.9%	1993–1995	4.1%
1946–1995	4.8%	1970–1995	7.0%	1994–1995	4.7%
1947–1995	4.9%	1971–1995	7.0%	1995–1995	5.6%
1948–1995	5.0%	1972–1995	7.1%		
1949–1995	5.1%	1973–1995	7.2%		

> Treasuries have averaged about 4% a year over the long term.

Source: *SBBI 1996 Yearbook.* Chicago: Ibbotson Associates, 1996. Reprinted with permission.

EXHIBIT 2 – 8

US Treasury Bills—Total Return (1926–1995)

Calendar Year Total Return

Year	Return	Year	Return	Year	Return
1926	3.3%	1950	1.2%	1974	8.0%
1927	3.1%	1951	1.5%	1975	5.8%
1928	3.6%	1952	1.7%	1976	5.1%
1929	4.7%	1953	1.8%	1977	5.1%
1930	2.4%	1954	0.9%	1978	7.2%
1931	1.1%	1955	1.6%	1979	10.4%
1932	1.0%	1956	2.5%	1980	11.2%
1933	0.3%	1957	3.1%	1981	14.7%
1934	0.2%	1958	1.5%	1982	10.5%
1935	0.2%	1959	3.0%	1983	8.8%
1936	0.2%	1960	2.7%	1984	9.8%
1937	0.3%	1961	2.1%	1985	7.7%
1938	0.0%	1962	2.7%	1986	6.2%
1939	0.0%	1963	3.1%	1987	5.5%
1940	0.0%	1964	3.5%	1988	6.3%
1941	0.1%	1965	3.9%	1989	8.4%
1942	0.3%	1966	4.8%	1990	7.8%
1943	0.3%	1967	4.2%	1991	5.6%
1944	0.3%	1968	5.2%	1992	3.5%
1945	0.3%	1969	6.6%	1993	2.9%
1946	0.4%	1970	6.5%	1994	3.9%
1947	0.5%	1971	4.4%	1995	5.6%
1948	0.8%	1972	3.8%		
1949	1.1%	1973	6.9%		

☐ = Loss Year

# of Years = 70

# of Loss Years = 0

Note: Treasury bills did not pay any interest during the war years (1938–1941).

Source: *SBBI 1996 Yearbook.* Chicago: Ibbotson Associates, 1996. Reprinted with permission.

EXHIBIT 2 – 9

Inflation—Total Return (1926–1995)

Calendar Year Total Return

Year	Return		Year	Return
1926	−1.5%		1950	5.8%
1927	−2.1%		1951	5.9%
1928	−1.0%		1952	0.9%
1929	0.2%		1953	0.6%
1930	−6.0%		1954	−0.5%
1931	−9.5%		1955	0.4%
1932	−10.3%		1956	2.9%
1933	0.5%		1957	3.0%
1934	2.0%		1958	1.8%
1935	3.0%		1959	1.5%
1936	1.2%		1960	1.5%
1937	3.1%		1961	0.7%
1938	−2.8%		1962	1.2%
1939	−0.5%		1963	1.6%
1940	1.0%		1964	1.2%
1941	9.7%		1965	1.9%
1942	9.3%		1966	3.4%
1943	3.2%		1967	3.0%
1944	2.1%		1968	4.7%
1945	2.3%		1969	6.1%
1946	18.2%		1970	5.5%
1947	9.0%		1971	3.4%
1948	2.7%		1972	3.4%
1949	−1.8%		1973	8.8%

Year	Return
1974	12.2%
1975	7.0%
1976	4.8%
1977	6.8%
1978	9.0%
1979	13.3%
1980	12.4%
1981	8.9%
1982	3.9%
1983	3.8%
1984	4.0%
1985	3.8%
1986	1.1%
1987	4.4%
1988	4.4%
1989	4.6%
1990	6.1%
1991	3.1%
1992	2.9%
1993	2.7%
1994	2.7%
1995	2.7%

# of Years = 70

of *Deflation* Years
= 10, or 14.3%

= Deflation

Source: *SBBI 1996 Yearbook*. Chicago: Ibbotson Associates, 1996. Reprinted with permission.

Now the important issue is to consider the erosion of purchasing power that inflation takes from your investments.
Exhibit 2–10 reveals the long-term rates of inflation. The
chart at the lower portion of Exhibit 2–10 reveals how much
this erosion impacts your investment return each year. Just
subtract the rate of inflation from your investment returns to
get an idea of the real rate of return of the asset classes just
discussed.

Is it a coincidence that both inflation and Treasury bills are
both near 4 percent over the long term? Not a chance! It
points to our second basic investment principle—that **inflation grows at about 4 percent a year and the government prices T-bills to correspond with inflation.**

WHAT IS A "REAL RATE OF RETURN"?

The real rate of return is earnings minus the effects of inflation. This reflects the real purchasing power of your gain.
What do you find when we examine the asset classes after
inflation and look at the "real rate of return"? There are negative periods, but through the long term, stocks provide a 6
percent real rate of return. This is how that number is
derived: During the long term, stocks pay 10 percent, and
inflation is 4 percent, so we subtract inflation.

What is the lesson here? If an investor wants to improve his
standard of living and keep above inflation, he needs to own
stocks. If a person keeps his money in Treasury bills, for the
long term, he only keeps even with the rate of inflation.
Bonds, with an average rate of return of 5 percent, leave
investors with a real rate of return of only 1 percent after
inflation. What does the entrepreneur want? Is it really any
different than what the average investor wants or do entrepreneurs go about it differently? Before answering these
questions, we need to take a closer look at the motivating
forces behind inflation and the entire economy.

EXHIBIT 2-10

Inflation
Total Annualized Return for Period Ending 1995

Time Period	Return	Time Period	Return	Time Period	Return	Time Period	Return	Time Period	Return
1926–1995	3.1%	1940–1995	4.4%	1954–1995	4.2%	1968–1995	5.5%	1982–1995	3.6%
1927–1995	3.2%	1941–1995	4.4%	1955–1995	4.4%	1969–1995	5.6%	1983–1995	3.6%
1928–1995	3.3%	1942–1995	4.3%	1956–1995	4.5%	1970–1995	5.6%	1984–1995	3.5%
1929–1995	3.3%	1943–1995	4.3%	1957–1995	4.5%	1971–1995	5.6%	1985–1995	3.5%
1930–1995	3.4%	1944–1995	4.3%	1958–1995	4.5%	1972–1995	5.7%	1986–1995	3.5%
1931–1995	3.5%	1945–1995	4.3%	1959–1995	4.6%	1973–1995	5.8%	1987–1995	3.7%
1932–1995	3.7%	1946–1995	4.4%	1960–1995	4.7%	1974–1995	5.6%	1988–1995	3.7%
1933–1995	4.0%	1947–1995	4.1%	1961–1995	4.8%	1975–1995	5.3%	1989–1995	3.5%
1934–1995	4.0%	1948–1995	4.0%	1962–1995	4.9%	1976–1995	5.2%	1990–1995	3.4%
1935–1995	4.1%	1949–1995	4.0%	1963–1995	5.0%	1977–1995	5.2%	1991–1995	2.8%
1936–1995	4.1%	1950–1995	4.2%	1964–1995	5.1%	1978–1995	5.2%	1992–1995	2.8%
1937–1995	4.1%	1951–1995	4.1%	1965–1995	5.3%	1979–1995	4.9%	1993–1995	2.7%
1938–1995	4.2%	1952–1995	4.1%	1966–1995	5.4%	1980–1995	4.4%	1994–1995	2.7%
1939–1995	4.3%	1953–1995	4.2%	1967–1995	5.5%	1981–1995	3.9%	1995–1995	2.7%

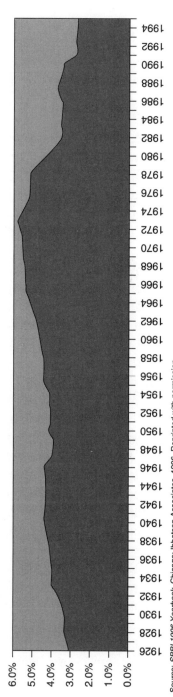

Source: *SBBI 1996 Yearbook.* Chicago: Ibbotson Associates, 1996. Reprinted with permission.

23

THE 4–4–4–4 PRINCIPLE

Inflation is here to stay as long as the U.S. dollar is not based on a gold standard. Inflation is built into the current economic policies of the United States Federal Reserve and the United States government monetary polices. The basics of the American economy are "4–4–4–4," the Equilibrium principle mentioned in the first chapter. The United States government and its agent, the Federal Reserve, want the economy to grow at 4 percent a year. They want inflation to grow at 4 percent a year. They want the money supply to grow at 4 percent a year, and they want interest rates to be at 4 percent a year. Why?

When the United States government borrows money, it issues a bond that guarantees payment in full in 20 or 30 years. During that 30-year period, the government prints more money and expands the money supply by 4 percent a year. Because there are 4 percent more dollars printed each year, the inflation rate is destined to be about 4 percent a year.

Why is the U.S. government doing this? Simple; the government does not have to pay back as much "real" money as it borrows. Over 25 years with 4 percent inflation, paying back a million dollars takes only $380,000 worth of purchasing power. Get it? (See Exhibit 2–11.)

> Simple; the government does not have to pay back as much "real" money as it borrows.

Money supply and interest rates are tools that the federal government can control. These are called the *controlling market forces* of the Federal Reserve.

There are free market forces out there. Yes, these free market forces are the entrepreneurs creating supply to meet demand so that entrepreneurs can extract a profit. *These free market forces* impact the inflation rate and the gross domestic product, or the economic growth rate.

Decline in Purchasing Power at 4 Percent Inflation

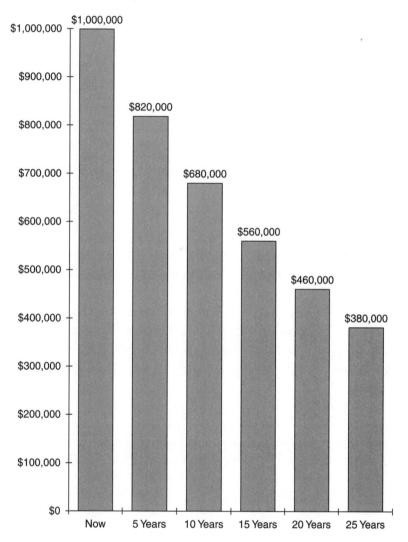

These are part of the regular U.S. business cycle. In an ideal world under this policy, everything grows at 4 percent a year and our economy should grow at 4 percent forever. But it doesn't—because of the free enterprise business opportunity. This is shown as step 1 in Exhibit 2–12.

EXHIBIT 2-12

Equilibrium

	Business Free Market Force		Federal Reserve Controlling Market Force		
	Inflation	GDP	Money Supply	Interest Rate	
Step 1.	4%	4%	4%	4%	IDEAL
Step 2.	↑ 4½	↑ 5	↓ 3	↑ 5	
Step 3.	↑ 4¾	↑ 5½	↓ 2	↑ 6	
Step 4.	↓ 4½	↓ 5	↑ 3	↓ 5	
Step 5.	4	4	4	4	

Because of the free market variables, the U.S. economy experiences business cycles. The portion of the business cycle we in the United States experienced in 1994 is called "disarray." 1995 was the boom effect of declining interest rates. 1996 should be "normal." If everything were perfect, everything would be in conformity. But because you cannot control all business entrepreneurs at all times, here is what unfolds.

Let's look at how the controlling market force (the Federal Reserve) uses its tools of money supply (MS) and interest rates (i) to put pressure on free market forces—inflation (I) and productivity (GNP). (See Exhibit 2–12.) The U.S. economy had come out of a recession in the 1992–93 years and therefore has stored-up demand caused by delayed purchases.

People had delayed purchasing a new car or a washing machine or TV because they were insecure about their financial future. Once the economy started to emerge from the recession, people began feeling more comfortable about the future, and they started buying again, especially durable goods, for example, televisions, cars, and so on. The economy heated up, and instead of growing at 4 percent in 1994, it began to grow at 5 percent because free enterprise producers met demand—"make hay while the sun shines!"

As soon as the economy started growing at 5 percent, what happened? The American worker reacted: "The American business owner/entrepreneur is making more profit. I want higher wages and if you don't give them to me voluntarily, I'll go on strike." Caterpillar and General Motors employees went on strike, among others. For what? Higher wages.

When workers are paid higher wages, what does that create? More security to release more pent-up demand, which can create more inflation. Because the economy is growing faster, inflation is growing faster and the entrepreneur is supplying products to meet demand.

What do the United States government and the Federal Reserve do? They want equilibrium. So the Federal Reserve raises interest rates to 5 percent and decreases the money supply as its method of forcing compliance. Instead of growing the money at 4 percent, the Federal Reserve (Fed) slows it to 3 percent growth. All this has happened in step 2 in a series of moves.

Like a teenager who does not listen to his parents the first time they say, "Be home at 10 o'clock," to test the boundaries, business continues to "make hay while the sun shines" and meet demand. As long as people want to buy TVs and cars, industry produces them. So, the economy may continue to grow (5½ percent) and inflation may continue to go even higher. What is the Fed going to do to restore equilibrium? To slow demand? They reduce the money supply to 2 percent and raise the interest rates to 6 percent. (This is shown in step 3.)

Eventually, what occurs is that control is gained by the Fed and things begin to return to normal. In a normal business cycle, when the economy starts to heat up, the cost of money becomes more expensive and the economy begins to get back in line because it costs more to buy credit—as costs of business increase, profits decrease. Prices are raised to restore profit and eventually demand is reduced by satisfaction or because prices are too high; only then will business growth decline (5 percent) and inflation drop to a lower rate, that is, inflation drops to 4.5 percent and the Fed responds by decreasing interest rates to 5 percent. (See Step 4.) Since the economy continues to slow, the Fed increases the money supply back to 3 and drops interest rates back to 5, and the economy starts to get back into equilibrium. Soon we are back to equilibrium—Step 5—and the business cycle is complete. Equilibrium is temporarily restored. Now that you understand free and controlling market forces, it is time to look at a business cycle (see Exhibit 2–13).

EXHIBIT 2–13

Idealized Business Cycle and Six Business Cycle Stages

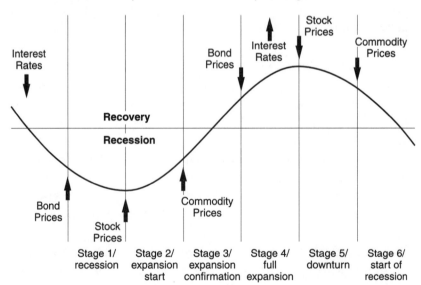

A TYPICAL BUSINESS CYCLE AND WHAT YOU SHOULD DO AT EACH STAGE

Stage 1 of the business cycle is the stage where the economy is in a recession and people are being laid off jobs. There is a slowdown in the economy. It is not growing at 4 percent. So, what does the Federal Reserve do? They drop interest rates. This was the case in 1995.

The number one tool to prime the pump is to drop interest rates. The Federal Reserve does this to make it easier to create business and easier to make profits. If you are a business owner and you obtain money to finance your inventory at virtually no cost, you are much more willing to take that risk.

Why do you need to know this? When interest rates decrease, what happens to stocks? They go up in value. Why? Safe investments like CDs that were paying 6 percent with the guarantee of no growth now compete with stocks, such as utilities, with a 6 percent dividend. The dividend can go up, and so can the stock price. Secondly, if companies pay less in interest expense, they can then direct the money saved to more profitable ventures and increase profits.

You should buy in anticipation of stocks going up in value. The typical investor waits a year until earnings are "confirmed"—a major mistake that the **Monster** wants you to make. (The Monster is what I affectionately call the market gremlin, who reveals himself as fear or greed.)

Stage Two of the business cycle takes place in the recession when the Fed is supplying businesses with cheaper money to prime the pump. Business entrepreneurs invest in new inventory, and produce items to sell in anticipation of stored-up demand being released. When items are produced to sell, business hires employees. When businesses are hiring, investment psychology improves. The outlook is positive. (1995 saw an S&P 500 return of 37.5 percent.)

Stage Two is potential earnings recognition from decreasing interest rates. Still in a recession during Stage Two, still in an economic slowdown, but now some in the investment community perceive that companies are going to make more profits in the near future.

As stated, the government would like the U.S. economy to grow at exactly 4 percent, but what do we often see happen? Coming out of a recession, the economy grows faster because there is a lot of stored-up demand. The business owner must make hay while the sun shines and take advantage of the climate by supplying product. Now the economy starts to accelerate. Workers are re-employed, the economy expands—which begins Stage Three: confirmation of economic recovery.

In **Stage Three,** consumers buy even more durable goods like a second car, a washing machine for the ski chalet, and so forth. Stocks rise in value; growth stocks and cyclical stocks become the market darlings. This is where the typical investor begins to think about investing—yet still waits. The smart entrepreneur should add to his investments at this point.

Durable goods such as cars are made out of "commodities": steel, rubber, oil, copper, and silica. The price of commodities rises because demand increases. The economy is experiencing a full-blown recovery and, as always, tends to get ahead of the curve. So what happens when the economy is expanding too fast? The government's agent, the Fed, raises interest rates. This begins **Stage Four.** The entrepreneur is selling stocks that benefited from this growth phase and re-deploys the gains into more defensive stocks, or takes advantage of high interest rates, that is, buys more bank and finance stocks.

Bonds begin to decline in value. When interest rates are increasing and bonds are paying 10 percent rather than the previous 8 percent, the principal value on bonds must drop in value. Because interest rates are increasing as the Fed exerts control of the economy, what often happens as Stage Four progresses? Fear begins to inject itself into the investors' dreams—part of the Monster.

Rates are raised again, and again, and again. In 1994—seven increases! The cost of borrowing money becomes higher and the potential for profits for corporations becomes less. Some stock prices start to go down. The economy starts to slow down as the increases in interest rates curb demand, profits go down, businesses lay off workers—**Stage 5.** Fear is now the topic of the newscasters and headlines.

Stage 6 is recession—jobs are lost, homes foreclosed, bankruptcies—doom—fear—survival? The **Monster** fear is forcing sales of securities rather than purchases. The individual sells—the entrepreneur who has saved his profits gazes at the opportunity presented to him and takes advantage of the market lows.

During Stage 6, watch out for the "sharks." The price of everything declines—the typical investor surrenders to fear (sharks) and sells stocks. Who are the sharks? "Wall Street," headlines, advertisements, salesmen who are motivated to move your money and take a piece of it. All parasites of the Monster. Doom?—Gloom?—Crash? In 1995, after investors sold because of Orange County's bankruptcy and Mexico's devaluation—headlines predicted a crash. Shazam, the market went up 20 percent in the next six months—and up 37.5 percent for the year. Why? Because stocks were too cheap! The entrepreneur was buying at this point.

These are the six stages of an economic cycle and the sad tale of the average investor compared to the happier one of the savvy entrepreneur. The government's goal is to make this rising and falling as close to a flat line as possible. Depending on where the economy is in the cycle, bonds, stocks, and commodities are rising; or stocks and commodities are rising but bonds are going down; or commodities are rising but stocks and bonds are going down; or stocks and commodities are going down but bonds are rising; or they are all going down. Why does the average investor start chasing and reacting to the vagaries of the market, to his or her detriment? Wall Street's latest "new fund" can make up further losses overnight—just listen to the sales promo. As always, the individual investor succumbs to fear (a.k.a. sharks), in reality, the Monster Fear. The investment-savvy entrepreneur is adding to his portfolio because he understands this is just part of the cycle.

THE POINT IS

So why is this so important and how can this help you double the market? **If you know what stage the economy is in, in the business cycle, and you do not lose sight of where the next stage will appear, it is simple to determine which industries are going to participate in the rising or falling of the business cycle.**

As an example, in an economic slowdown, noncyclical blue-chip high-dividend companies do better than other types of companies. A noncyclical resists the impact of business cycles. A solid investment in a noncyclical could be a telephone or utility company that has a secure dividend, or a drug company that produces products that people must buy despite the economy. For instance, people cannot put off illness because of an economic cycle; if they are sick, people are going to buy their life-saving drugs.

As the slowdown and eventual recovery start to take effect, people buy stock in cyclical industries that have visible earnings such as automobile companies, and, yes, washing machines—durable goods that will be bought when stored-up demand is released.

In the expansionary cycle, cyclical and leveraged growth companies do well. And by the way, new underwritings flourish—for a time—something like a shooting star! Many are too weak to survive the next cycle and are often the first to plummet—a signal to the entrepreneur.

In the expansion peak, where there is high volatility, non-cyclical high-yield companies such as telephone or utilities are a good investment because of their attractive dividends in the face of declining interest rates. The cycle goes on.

In reality, a business cycle can be divided into more than six stages because there are a significant number of economic events in addition to financial market rotation. The purpose here is to provide you a reliable method of identifying which stage of the business cycle the economy is in and how certain industries will react to each cycle. Exhibit 2–14 summarizes the phases of the business cycle for you.

The business cycle has consistently repeated itself since the beginning of the 19th century, when reliable statistics first became available. A typical cycle averages closer to 3.6 years in length and encompasses an economic expansion and contraction. Some are slower; some are longer—hence the phrase that economists use: "3–5 year cycle." The contractionary phase normally takes the form of decline in the level of economic activity, that is, a recession, but sometimes it is limited to a slowdown in the rate of growth, known as a growth recession.

When an expansion is particularly long, that is, 6–10 years, it may include a growth recession. The United States is so large and diversified that it actually has as many as six

EXHIBIT 2-14

The Phases of the Business Cycle

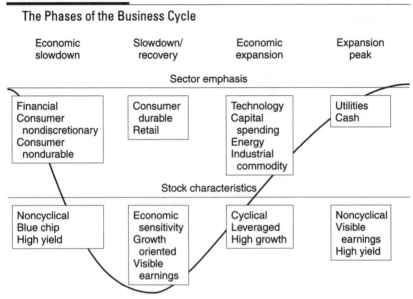

Economic slowdown	Slowdown/ recovery	Economic expansion	Expansion peak

Sector emphasis

| Financial Consumer nondiscretionary Consumer nondurable | Consumer durable Retail | Technology Capital spending Energy Industrial commodity | Utilities Cash |

Stock characteristics

| Noncyclical Blue chip High yield | Economic sensitivity Growth oriented Visible earnings | Cyclical Leveraged High growth | Noncyclical Visible earnings High yield |

different economies—for example, Auto, Midwest; Aerospace, California; Manufacturing, Southeast. A long expansion is usually separated into two mini-cycles. For example, the recovery that began in 1982 experienced a sharp slowdown in growth in 1984 and 1985, and actually contained two complete "mini" stock and commodity cycles.

Nevertheless, the primary trend of the stock market is always up. Yes, always up. The secondary short-term trend of the financial markets—bonds, stocks, and commodities—is determined by the business cycle, and the direction of

Nevertheless, the primary trend of the stock market is always up.

the trend depends on the maturity or stage of the prevailing cycle. A significant part of why my clients consistently double the market is because they can now identify business cycle sequences and stages.

How can you take advantage of this knowledge? Abandon fear, as you now know what entrepreneurs know but most investors **do not!** When the economy is in recession—Buy! Buy! Buy! Because your neighbor is selling, selling, selling!

NEXT STEP—HOW DO YOU KNOW IF THE MARKET IS CHEAP OR EXPENSIVE?

One of the most common fallacies is made by looking at the stock market and concluding from the numbers above that it is high or low. Rarely is it either dear or cheap. For example, in December 1991, the stock market as measured by the Dow Jones was at 3,169 points. The reason it was "high" is that, at that time, the price/earnings (P/E) multiple was at 24 times earnings. (Stay with me. I will explain.) What many investors did not recognize is that the stock market was beginning a silent crash. The stock market may go from 3,100 to 5,000, but at 5,000, it may be 40 percent cheaper than it was at 3,100 because it is only trading at 14 times earnings. (Hang in there. I'll be explaining P/E shortly.)

One of the biggest misunderstandings about the stock market is how it is valued. If the Dow Jones is at 6,000, what does that mean? Is it high, low, cheap, or overpriced? Do you really believe that your newscaster knows? As Tom Brokaw explained to me in Paris recently—the media rule is, "If it bleeds, it leads." In other words, give the public what it wants or someone else will. Unfortunately, the public relishes someone else's bad news—now you know a secret—the stock market climbs a wall of worry and slips in a time of glee.

Have you ever heard the term "price/earnings multiple (P/E)"? It is how you measure the value of a company. If a company is earning $1 a share and the public is buying stock at $10 a share, the market price is divided by the earnings.

In this case, 10 is divided by one; this tells us that the stock is selling at 10 times earnings (10 P/E or 10x). If you invested in this company and paid $10, theoretically you are paying 10 years' worth of earnings to own that company today.

However, the stock market has had a high and low band on stocks for many years. Typically, stock markets get very high and have difficulty getting much higher when the S&P 500 is at about 25 to 30 times earnings. Yes, there are exceptions, but this is a good general rule of thumb. Exhibit 2–15 shows the typical movement of stocks between the upper and lower bands.

EXHIBIT 2–15

Dow Jones Industrial Average P/E Multiples

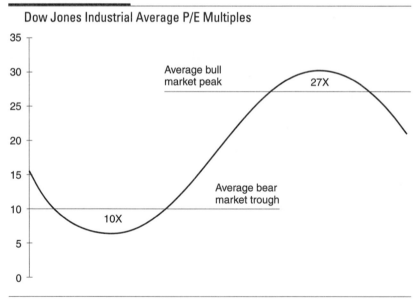

	Extreme Lows		Highs	
	1974	6.0	1933	51.5
	1980	6.2	1992	29.7
	1950	6.4	1991	29.2
	1979	6.4	1934	28.3
	1978	6.6	1938	26.4

Source: Duff Phelps Equity Research. Reprinted with permission.

When stock markets are low, they have difficulty going lower if they are about 10 times earnings. Let us give you an example. Say XYZ company has a market value at $10 a share. Its price/earnings multiple is 10 times (10x). A year from now, that company is still trading at $10 a share ("earnings per share"—EPS), but their earnings have gone to $2. What is its price/earnings (P/E) multiple? 10/2 = 5. Five! Is the stock a better value trading at five times than at 10 times? Bet it is—it is half as expensive as it used to be. Rarely does the market as a whole get lower than 10x.

What you must do is discard conventional thoughts about the number value of the Dow Jones or the S&P 500. This has no relationship to stock market valuation at all. Rid yourself of the fallacy of thinking about the value of the Dow Jones or the value of stocks expressed in terms of dollars. Dollars are only a measure, like pints or liters.

> What you must do is discard conventional thoughts about the number value of the Dow Jones or the S&P 500.

Let me give you just one example that will explain this important point. Back in December 1991 (see Exhibit 2–16), the stock market was trading at 3,169—24 times earnings. What happened was this: earnings per share (EPS) in 1992 went up 17 percent. In 1993, EPS again rose by 14 percent. In 1994, EPS went up another 15 percent. Add these three increases together, and the EPS shot up 46 percent in just three years.

But what has happened to the Dow Jones average since 1991? Not much. It went from 3,169 to 3,832 in 1994, but the P/E ratio actually went down from 24 to 14. When you examine the stock market in January 1994 it was extremely cheap— 14x earnings, 40 percent less than 1991—yet what were the

E X H I B I T   2 – 1 6

Price/Earnings Valuation

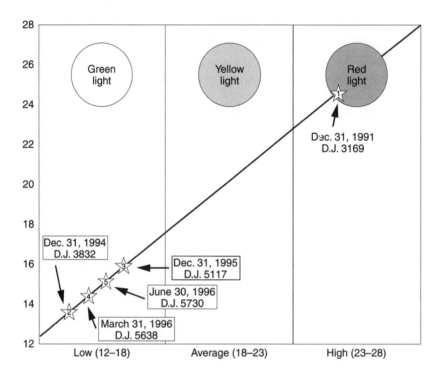

headlines?—"Crash"—"Bear Market Ahead"—Shazam, next stop is 6,400 as this book goes to press. The lesson—1,000, 2,000, 3,000, 4,000, 5,000 on the Dow means <u>nothing</u>.

Buying pressure forces the price of stocks to go up; selling pressure forces them down. In the absence of buying and selling pressure, what happens to the stock market? It stagnates—is boring—and the financial leaders/salesmen need to **make** news. So you will move your money and they can get a piece of it.

What keeps the stock market from going up? That's the next step—learning the fundamentals of investing in the next two chapters.

3

Advanced Fundamentals of Investing—Part One

As we've seen from the discussion in Chapter 2, common stocks average around 10 percent return a year, year in and year out. Everyone thinks that stocks possess a greater degree of "risk" than do bonds or Treasury bills.

When an investment is considered, an investor is normally concerned with the rate of return but often does not have any real ability to evaluate the risk. And even if he asks the question—does he really get the answer? When was the last time you **read** a prospectus, especially the last half? And if you ask about risk, what definition do you mean? The loss of principal or higher volatility? Risk is generally defined as loss of principal value, but there are a variety of types of risk,

among them volatility, market risk, business risk, currency
valuation, etc.

RISK/RETURN COMPARISON—A KEY TOOL
TO SUCCESSFUL INVESTING

It is for this reason most professional investment management consultants utilize a risk/return comparison and evaluate risk and volatility. Exhibit 3–1 is the fundamental tool
that you must use to analyze an investment opportunity.

Vertically, measure the rate of return—horizontally, measure
the rate of risk volatility. Everyone is aware that if you want
a high rate of return, you must be willing to accept a higher
rate of volatility. The purpose of this chart is to graphically
and statistically plot out how the basic asset classes have
done in a past period. Yes, you can compare apples, oranges,
grapes, and apricots. In this chart, you can compare any
class or style of mutual funds, investment manager, or index
to each other.

Common stocks have generally returned 10 percent but have
had greater quarterly volatility than bonds; government
bonds returned 5 percent but had greater quarterly volatility
than Treasury bills; and Treasury bills returned only 4 percent with very low volatility.

**Refer to this risk/return chart again and again
because it is one more tool needed to succeed.** If your
investment advisor, mutual fund 800 number, CPA, and so
on, do not have this chart, fire them immediately and tell
them **not** to come back until they know what the volatility is
and the return is and how the ratio of the two relates to your
specific needs.

Historical Ranges of Returns and Risk for Various Investment Strategies
Period of 1926–1994

The annualized rate of returns expressed vertically while the variability (risk) is expressed horizontally in terms of quarter-to-quarter variation. The line connecting Treasury bills and the S&P 500 is the capital market return line. As one incurs more risk, one should achieve a greater return to compensate for that risk.

The areas numbered 1 through 6 indicate the expected range of return and risk for each of the following asset categories.

1. CPI Inflation rates
2. Cash or Money Market Investments
3. Bond or Fixed Income Investments
4. Balanced (Stocks, and Bond Investments)
5. Long-Term Growth Equity
6. Maximum Growth Equity Investments

The return and risk may not fall in these indicated areas on an annual basis; however, over longer periods of time these are the expected results of the seven investment categories.

1926–1994

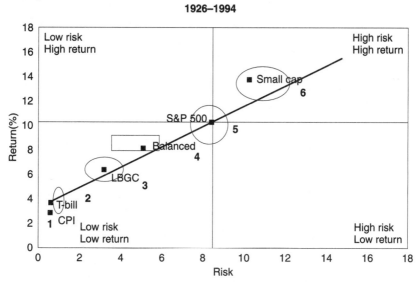

Source: *SBBI Yearbook 1995.* Chicago: Ibbotson Associates, 1995. Reprinted with permission.

Exhibit 3–2 is a variation on the previous risk/return chart; this shows the risk/return analysis for a five-year period of various asset classes, indexes, and specific portfolios. Use the S&P 500 index as the baseline. The chart is divided in half, top to bottom, showing returns greater or lesser than the S&P 500. Right to left, the chart is divided for greater or lesser volatility than the S&P 500. Why have you not seen this chart? Every broker, insurance agent, mutual fund, and investment advisor has access to this—it is probably marked "internal use only." We will discuss this in more detail in Chapter 7.

The line running from Treasury bills diagonally is *not* a risk/ return line; it is an "investment expectation" line. What it tells us is that if you are willing to incur a greater degree of volatility, you can expect a higher rate of return. It is a given

EXHIBIT 3–2

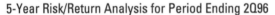

5-Year Risk/Return Analysis for Period Ending 2Q96

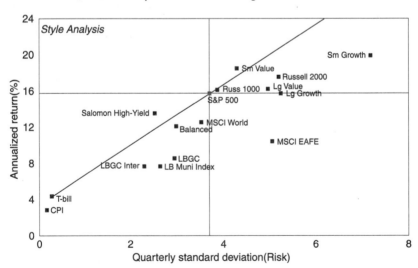

that the reward will be there only if you stay invested. This concept will become very important to you later on, as you shall see.

We call this volatility "standard deviation." Standard deviation is a measure of volatility around the mean. For those of you who are more statistically inclined, look in the glossary to see how this works. Standard deviation is considered by many in the financial services industry to be *the* measure of risk.

Let us also take a look at the chart another way. We know the historical rates of return. If we were to invest $1 in each of these various asset classes during the period 1926–94 and track their volatility, here is what would have happened. (See Exhibit 3–3.)

EXHIBIT 3–3

History of Investment Performance, 1925–1995

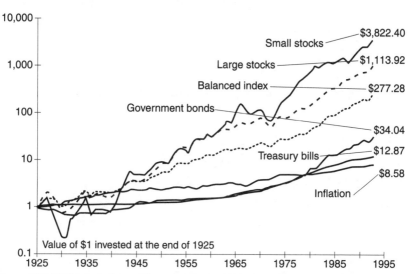

Source: *SBBI 1996 Yearbook.* Chicago: Ibbotson Associates, 1996. Reprinted with permission.

One dollar from the 71-year period 1925 to 1995 invested with a rate of return of inflation would have grown to $8.58. One dollar in Treasury bills grew to $12.87. You can see that putting your money in Treasury bills would have kept you a little ahead of inflation over this period of time. But now look closely at the 18-year period since 1977.

The difference between 5 percent and 4 percent more than *doubles* your net worth through those years. Bonds at an average of 5 percent have grown to $34.04, more than two times the worth of Treasury bills. You will also notice, however, that a slightly higher rate of volatility is expressed by the lack of evenness in this line.

> The staggering difference of compounding at 10 percent versus 5 percent over a long-term period is significant to your net worth.

Take a look at some other investments. If you put your money in the large stocks, one dollar grew to $1,113.92—more than 30 times the net worth bonds produced, and more than 80 times the net worth Treasury bills produced. **The staggering difference of compounding at 10 percent versus 5 percent over a long-term period is significant to your net worth.**

TAKING ADVANTAGE OF COMPOUNDING— THE LIFE-CYCLE INVESTMENT ALLOCATION MODEL

Why is this long-term compounding important to you and how can you put it to use? Each one of us is involved, like it or not, in a life-cycle and on average we tend to retire by age 65. Actuarial tables indicate that if a person is 65 and healthy, he or she is likely to live to be more than 80. For most of us, we must plan our investments through a life-cycle spanning a period of some 80 to 90 years. Because of medicine today, 90 years or even 100 years of life could be achievable by the end of this century.

Time is the single most important variable in the History of Investment Performance chart. As people age, salaries and income increase. The obligations of raising children and putting them through school are also increasing. Discretionary income increases but life expectancy decreases. What do we do about this?

My answer? I developed a life-cycle investment allocation model that enables you to most effectively capture the benefits of compounding. (See Exhibit 3–4.)

This should be your guide: When most investors are 25 years old, my advice is to put 90 percent of their money into common stock and 10 percent in balanced accounts. Why is this advisable? Because at a minimum, they have 40 years until retirement and maybe 30 years beyond that. Twenty-five-year-old investors have the benefit of a lot of time ahead of them—maybe 70 or more years.

But as a person ages, the luxury of time diminishes. By the time a person is 45 years old, only 65 percent of his or her assets should be in stocks. The other 35 percent should be in balanced accounts that include stocks and bonds. Too often, people at age 60 want all bonds. That is the wrong approach, but it is what most self-managers do. We know that a person 60 years old still has a life expectation of 15 to 20, and possibly even 30, years.

As people age they gradually change their investment process. They have been adding to their investment pool for a number of years. At retirement, it is time to call on the asset pool for distribution. Instead of accumulating investments, as a worker, the retiree begins to "consume" investment to fulfill a comfortable retirement. Since we begin to conserve

EXHIBIT 3 – 4

Model Investor Life Cycle Asset Allocation

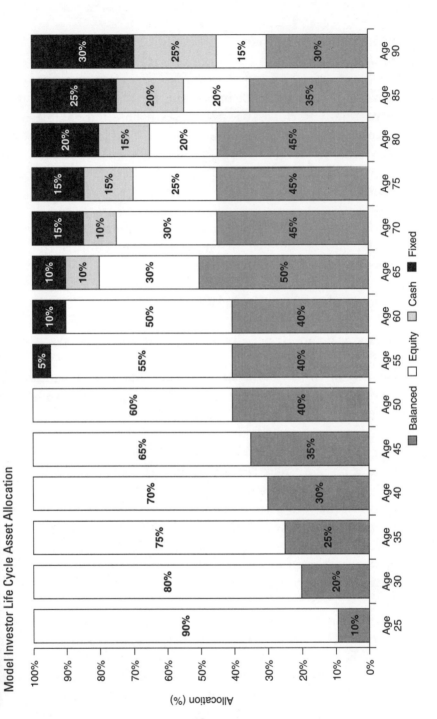

our investment pool each year at retirement, it helps to think of money in terms of consumption blocks. Let me give an example. Have two years' worth of your paycheck income invested in a liquid class, such as the money markets, Treasury bills, or CDs. This amount assures you of enough funds for your immediate consumption needs and acts as a guarantee of income so you are less likely to sell longer-term, less-liquid assets out of fear. You can then allocate your other assets to classes generally considered more risky, such as stocks, and avoid the tendency to want to time the market. This is overall a much less risky strategy than indiscriminately pulling money out and then putting it back in the markets. Let me explain why this is so.

We all know from the studies we have seen thus far that stocks produce both a greater rate of return and higher volatility than bonds. Many people think that the least risk is having all their money in bonds. That is not true, as we will learn by examining the risk/return curve. Please note that I have included the ages of the model investor Asset Life-Cycle Asset Allocation along with the Allocation Risk/Reward Formula.

EXHIBIT 3-5

Historical Risk/Return Analysis

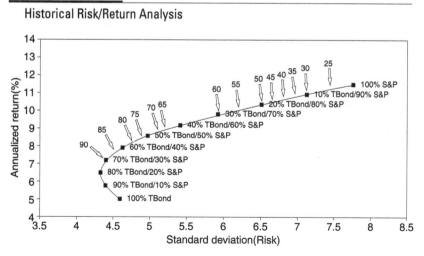

Risk/return analysis also reflects the relative return and volatility of various asset allocation strategies. Look at what is true. You find that there is actually little additional risk by being invested 50/50, with half your money in stocks and half in bonds, but the rate of return is 70 percent more than being 100 percent in bonds—a 7 to 1 reward/risk ratio. (See Exhibit 3–5.)

So many of the assumed "fundamentals" about investing are merely myths. They are neither scientific nor based on truth. Often, they have been told to you by a friend, "banker," or insurance agent. Wait to see how things have changed in the '90s!

The big myth is that the stock market is impacted by news events. **LIE!** The number one excuse for delaying investment decisions is current events high- lighted in the news. This is the major reason why individuals don't invest at a particular time.

The big myth is that the stock market is impacted by news events. LIE!

Exhibit 3–6 depicts the major news items on a year-by-year basis and how the S&P 500 grew over the 60- year period. No matter what the headlines show, look at the direction of the S&P 500!

For example, consider the Great Depression, the Kennedy assassination, the Cuban missile crisis, and so forth. I reiter- ate! News events have *absolutely no impact* on the stock market. Please explore and look at this historically. The blips you see are business cycles—just that.

Many people think that the political climate impacts invest- ments. But if one takes a look at the stock market post–World

EXHIBIT 3-6

There Are Always "Reasons" Not to Invest

1934 Depression
1935 Spanish Civil War
1936 Economy still struggling
1937 Recession
1938 War clouds gather
1939 War in Europe
1940 France falls
1941 Pearl Harbor
1942 Wartime price controls
1943 Industry mobilizes
1944 Consumer goods shortage
1945 Post-war recession predicted
1946 Dow tops 200—market too high
1947 Cold war begins
1948 Berlin blockade
1949 Russia explodes A-bomb
1950 Korean War
1951 Excess Profits Tax
1952 U.S. seizes steel mills
1953 Russia explodes H-bomb
1954 Dow tops 300—market too high
1955 Eisenhower illness
1956 Suez crisis
1957 Russia launches Sputnik
1958 Recession
1959 Castro seizes power in Cuba
1960 Russia downs U-2 plane
1961 Berlin wall erected
$100
1962 Cuban missile crisis
1963 Kennedy assassinated

S&P 500
$65,705.00

1964 Gulf of Tonkin
1965 Civil rights marches
1966 Vietnam War escalates
1967 Newark race riots
1968 *USS Pueblo* seized
1969 Money tightens—market falls
1970 Cambodia invaded–Vietnam War spreads
1971 Wage price freeze
1972 Largest US trade deficit ever
1973 Energy crisis
1974 Steepest market drop in four decades
1975 Clouded economic prospects
1976 Economic recovery slows
1977 Market slumps
1978 Interest rates rise
1979 Oil prices skyrocket
1980 Interest rates at all-time high
1981 Steep recession begins
1982 Worst recession in 40 years
1983 Market hits new highs
1984 Record federal deficit
1985 Economic growth slows
1986 Dow nears 2000
1987 Record-setting market decline
1988 Election year
1989 October "mini-crash"
1990 Persian Gulf crisis
1991 Communism falls
1992 Political uncertainty
1993 Soft landing?
1994 Rising interest rates
1995 Orange County bankrupt/Peso

Source: *SBBI 1995 Yearbook*. Chicago: Ibbotson Associates, 1995. Reprinted with permission.

War II, one finds that when the Republicans were in power, there was a U.S. recession an average of once every 4.7 years — and when the Democrats were in power, there was a U.S. recession once every 5.3 years. Returns were 11.8 percent per year and 11.2 percent per year, respectively. Politics do not, in fact, have a significant impact on the business cycle or investment returns. (See Exhibit 3–7.)

EXHIBIT 3-7

Stock Prices and Recessions
(Data Below President's Names Are S&P 500 Compound Growth Rates)

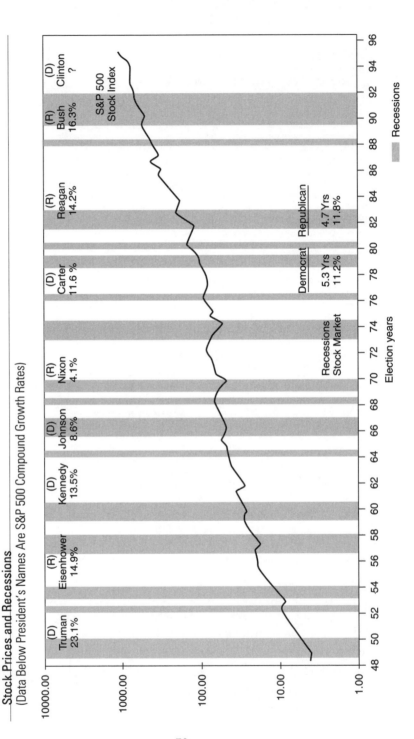

THE FALLACY OF TIMING THE MARKET

Most people think that they can improve their performance by market timing. As I showed you in my second tip in the Introduction, this is not so! Take a look at just how impossible this is. Many people perceived the 1980s to be one of the best decades ever. The S&P 500's return compounded at 17.5 percent. However, if you missed the best 40 trading days of the total 2,528 trading days of that decade, you only made 3.9 percent. (See Exhibit 3–8.)

At a 17.5 percent return, the 1980s *were* very good years for the stock market. However, take a different look at the 1980s based on "headlines" and major news events. The United States started the decade with the highest interest rates ever recorded in history, compounded by the highest inflation this country has ever experienced, leading us into the worst recession since the Depression. The second largest stock market crash in history occurred in 1987, followed two years later by the third largest stock market crash. We had Resolution Trust Corp. (designed by the federal government to dispose of defaulted S&L property) brought to you by the Tax Reform Act of 1986. And at the end of the decade we went to war. In spite of all that, the stock market continued climbing. Why? Because, as we also discussed in the first and second chapters, political events do not have a far-reaching

EXHIBIT 3–8

Missing a Few Good Days Substantially Reduces Return

1980–1989	S&P 500 Annualized Return*
All 2,528 trading days:	17.50%
Minus 10 best days:	12.60%
Minus 20 best days:	9.30%
Minus 30 best days:	6.50%
Minus 40 best days:	3.90%

*Figures assume that when not invested in stocks, assets were earning interest at the average rate of 30-day Treasury bills over the 1980–1989 period.
Source: Datastream, Ibbotson Associates, and Sanford C. Bernstien Co. Reprinted with permission.

impact on the market, nor do isolated economic events. The key factors are the business cycle and the basic fundamental condition of the markets; *these* are the keys on which to gauge the market. Growth of business tends to be exponential, and where there is a problem or opportunity, businesses will find a way to get solutions—regardless of what the day's headlines report.

Market timing and stock swapping are, at best, very difficult challenges. The only way to know if it has been a good trading day is, after it is over and you get home, to listen while Dan, Tom, or Peter reports on the evening news just how much the Dow 30 Industrials are up or down.

> ## Market timing and stock swapping are, at best, very difficult challenges.

The investment principle to remember here is: *Be in the market at all times to win.* Stay invested—you'll reap the rewards of compounding *and* you won't miss out on any of those very valuable high days. Your program will stay on track and you can be assured of good returns over the long term while the average investor panics and decimates his or her investment plan.

Don't rely on stock selection, market timing, or second guessing. Knowing that you have to be in, how can you mitigate your risk? This is the subject of the next chapter: the secrets of "value investing."

4

CHAPTER

Advanced Fundamentals of Investing—Part Two

Now that we've seen the importance of gauging performance based on the risk/reward analysis and highlighted the importance of staying fully invested, let's continue to learn how to double the market. Our focus in this chapter will be on how to mitigate the risks associated with investing. We'll start by looking at the two basic styles of investing, "value investing" and "growth investing." Most money managers use one or the other, or a combination of the two. Becoming familiar with these two investment styles can give you a definite edge, as you'll soon see.

VALUE INVESTING

Value investing is a term developed by Graham and Dodd in their noted research book,

Fundamentals of Investing. Like its name implies, value investing seeks out the company whose fundamental value is considered better than others in its industry. Benjamin Graham popularized the notion of "buying a dollar for $0.50" as a way to reduce downside risk. Utilizing 18 key financial ratios and evaluating balance sheets of many different corporations, Graham was able to determine a company's fundamental value when compared to other similar companies in the same industry. Dividends are an important part of value investing. Value investing means you buy large companies with big dividends that are "cheap" in terms of price/earnings multiples.

Here are the four basic historic principles of value investing:

1. Invest when the earnings yield on the stock is twice the prevailing AAA bond yield.
2. Invest when the dividend yield is 2/3 or more the AAA bond yield.
3. Buy a stock if the dividend yield is higher than that of the S&P 500 average by a factor of 10 percent (e.g., S&P 500 average dividend = 3.0 percent, candidate stock dividend = 3.3 percent).
4. Buy a stock if the price earnings multiple is 1/2 that of the S&P 500.

GROWTH INVESTING

The alternative investment philosophy is "growth investing." This form of investing places more emphasis on the future growth potential of a company. Growth investors will often evaluate the financial ratio and balance sheet data of a particular company, but they also look at developing trends such as increasing market share, new products coming to market, expansion plans, change in management, and so forth. New products and changes tend to have a future impact on companies; growth stocks tend to have a higher price/earnings multiple than value stocks. Companies that are looking forward are often investing in new technology and expansion, and their earnings are reinvested in the company for growth of the company rather than paid out in the form of dividends.

These are the classic descriptions of growth and value and their main differences. But when should you own value stocks or growth stocks?

THE BUSINESS CYCLE AND VALUE AND GROWTH STYLES

Many investors fail to understand the performance of their stocks because they are unaware of where the economy is in the business cycle. Over a period of time, there is a contra-cyclical wave action between value and growth style, as you can see in Exhibit 4–1.

> Many investors fail to understand the performance of their stocks because they are unaware of where the economy is in the business cycle.

When studying the stock market, we find there are periods of time when value stocks do well and other times when they do worse than the general market. We find that there are periods of time when the converse is true of growth stocks.

Historical evidence shows that there is a particular time to own value stocks and a time to own growth stocks. A time to reap and a time to sow. And yes, it is tied to the business cycle we discussed in Chapter 2, as you can see in the following chart. (See Exhibit 4–2.)

During an economic slowdown and recovery period (Stages One, Two, and Three), you will get a better return than the

E X H I B I T   4 – 1

An Example of the Cycles of Styles

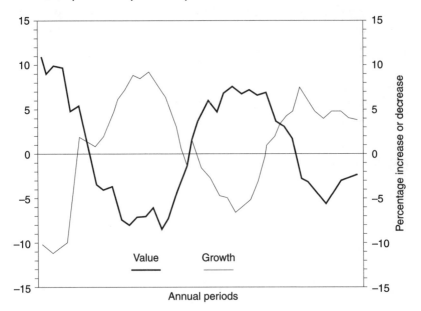

E X H I B I T   4 – 2

Peaks and Troughs of the Financial Markets as They Relate
to the Business Cycle

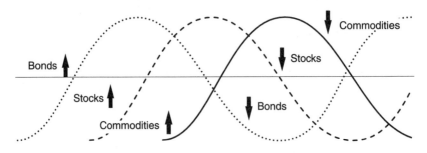

The Business Cycle and Growth and Value Stock Cycles

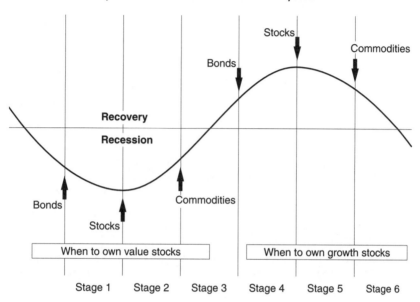

general market by owning value stocks. (See Exhibit 4–3.) In Stages Four and Five of the business cycle, growth stocks tend to do better than value stocks. However, it is interesting to note that for the long term, they tend to do about the same.

Most investors and even money managers have a tendency to chase recently posted track records rather than take advantage of the growth and value cycles. One of the biggest pitfalls is investing based on last year's track record; just because value stocks performed well last year does not mean they are going to perform well this year. This is another reason to know your business cycle and its different stages.

GROWTH AND VALUE PERFORMANCE VERSUS THE S&P 500

We tracked the performance of growth stocks and value stocks for a three-year period relative to the S&P 500. In all cases, we found out the following: growth stocks have higher volatility than the S&P 500 at all times. Value stocks have lower volatility than the S&P 500 most of the time. About half the time, growth stocks did better than the S&P 500

> Growth stocks have higher volatility than the S&P 500 at all times.

and half the time value stocks did better than the S&P 500.

However, if you had a portfolio divided equally between value stocks and growth stocks, a very interesting thing happens. *Portfolios that were allocated 50 percent in value stocks and 50 percent growth always beat the market and always had lower volatility.* How can this be? Part of this is that the S&P also has other types of stocks in it besides value and growth; it has utilities, telephones, transportation, and so on. Another reason is that value stocks have higher-than-average dividends than the S&P 500.

DIVERSIFICATION BETWEEN VALUE STOCKS AND GROWTH STOCKS

Another basic secret of investing, therefore, is to divide your portfolio equally between value stocks and growth stocks. Academic research, conducted by David Herman, found that the lowest P/E (value) stocks tend to do better than high P/E growth stocks over time. Since the average investor, unlike large institutions, is unable to conduct extensive research to find the most undervalued value stocks, such studies are more academically interesting than they are practical. Studies also show a tendency to underperform the market half the time and overperform it half the time. Your goal is to overperform the market all the time. And one of the secrets of how to do this is to blend these two styles: growth and value. You do this by changing, or "tilting" the allocation by 10 percent one way or the other, depending on where we are in the business cycle.

There are some easy ways to determine where we are in this cycle. Different independent associations publish the performance of growth and value stocks. The Russell Group publishes one; Wilshire publishes another.

You can use these charts to visually see where the trends are. An easy way to focus is to look at the stock group that has been underperforming for the longest period of time.

It is often best, however, to utilize the assistance of a professional investment advisor who has this data at his fingertips to help you. Different styles of investment advisors can be found through your financial advisor or certain mutual fund services.

Now, where do we stand today in the business cycle? Growth is the place to tilt your portfolio as this book is being written.

Growth stocks have underperformed for a period of time, and value stocks have overperformed for a period of time. This was caused by economic uncertainty. An observable shift to growth stocks occurred in the secnd quarter of 1996, signaling a shift to the growth phase of the market. (See Exhibit 4–4.)

STRATEGIC ASSET ALLOCATION—COMBINING ASSET AND STYLE ALLOCATIONS

In the industry, we call this blending of value and growth stocks "style allocation." It's a lot like asset allocation. While asset allocation is simply the way our money is divided up and weighted among different investment classes—stocks, bonds, international stocks, real estate, and a growing list of newly developed investment vehicles—style allocation further subdivides a class—for example, stocks into value or growth, or bonds into long term or intermediate term. Style allocation adds protection and performance to your portfolio over and above the performance added by the investment advisors you

E X H I B I T   4 – 4

Summary of Styles & Indices

Description	2Q'96	1 YR	2YR	3YR	5YR	10YR
BIG						
S&P 500	4.54	25.99	26.03	17.22	15.73	13.82
Dow Jones	1.79	26.40	27.80	20.08	17.35	15.23
LG Growth*	7.55	29.68	30.47	19.03	15.69	14.42
LG Value*	0.54	25.74	23.44	13.80	16.05	13.85
MID						
MID Growth*	3.15	27.02	29.66	19.87	19.64	11.44
MID Value*	0.19	20.61	19.34	12.19	17.58	11.71
SMALL						
Russell 2000	5.00	23.91	21.97	15.81	17.51	10.40
SM Growth*	5.57	25.50	30.62	19.69	19.82	11.65
SM Value*	1.42	19.73	17.29	11.87	18.42	13.25
FOREIGN						
EAFE	1.66	13.62	7.63	10.76	10.34	10.58
World	3.01	18.99	15.04	13.60	12.53	11.60
FIXED						
LBGC	0.47	4.65	8.63	5.16	8.48	8.41
T-Bill	1.27	5.49	5.37	4.63	4.44	5.85
CPI	0.80	2.71	2.84	2.70	2.82	3.67

Source: P.I.P.E.R./*Wilshire Indexes. Reprinted with permission.

choose and the stocks they buy, and adds greater protection than simply being 1/2 in stocks and 1/2 in bonds.

Research has demonstrated that, of all factors, asset allocation has perhaps the single greatest influence on your investment returns. Staying fully invested for the long term lets you realize the returns, but it is style allocation that adds that extra percentage in return and the decrease in volatility that

> Asset allocation has perhaps the single greatest influence on your investment returns.

help you deal with the fear during economic disarray, so style allocation gives you that much more added protection.

There is a logical reason why asset allocation makes you more money. It is called diversification. Diversification is simply spreading your investments among several asset classes. Diversification has long been known to lower the overall volatility of—or risk to—your portfolio.

The major investment categories include money market funds, certificates of deposit, bonds, domestic securities, real estate, foreign securities, and precious metals. A well-diversified portfolio will include investments in all of these areas. However, most individuals do not feel comfortable with all of these categories and will select several areas where they have the highest level of comfort. I personally avoid real estate and precious metals because of liquidity problems and high carrying costs. I have long ago concluded that "Happiness is a positive cash flow."

Diversification offers this benefit because each kind of investment follows a cycle all its own. Each asset responds differently to changes in the economy or the investment marketplace. If you own a variety of assets, a short-term decline in one can be balanced by others that are stable or going up.

As seen earlier, not all investment classes act the same. The stock market may go up one year and down the next, yet the bond market may remain unchanged. In this case, investors who owned both shares of a stock fund *and* shares of a bond fund will be better off than those who limited themselves to stocks only.

Suppose all your money is invested in stocks and you need to sell some of your holdings for an emergency. If stocks are depressed when you need to sell, you are forced to take a loss on your investment. Owning other investments would give you more flexibility in raising the needed cash while allowing you to hold your stocks until prices improve.

Money market funds can provide a foundation of stability and liquidity that is ideal for cash reserve. Bonds are good for steady, high income. Stocks have the greatest potential for superior long-term returns.

> Money market funds can provide a foundation of stability and liquidity that is ideal for cash reserve.

Let's look at some common myths. During a 25-year period of time, which has carried the most risk, stocks or bonds? In this question, risk is defined as loss of principal, loss of dollars at quarterly measurement points.

Let's look at Exhibit 4–5. For any 25 years, there have been 100 calendar quarters. If you had 100 percent of your money in the S&P 500, six times in the 25 years ending 1995, you would have lost between 0 and 1 percent in value—and six times, the market was down 2 to 3 percent. Two times it was down 3 to 4 percent. So 30 quarters out of the last 100 quarters, if you were 100 percent in the S&P 500, you would have lost value! What? Yes! How about bonds?

If you were 100 percent in bonds, 36 times out of the last 100 quarters, you lost value. If you were 100 percent in stocks, you would have met your expected return 21 times, but if you were 100 percent in bonds you would have met it 31 times.

How many times would you have done better than 4 percent per quarter? If you were 100 percent in stocks, you would have done better 49 times. If you were 100 percent in bonds, you would have done better 33 times.

So here is the truth of investing. You are better off being 100 percent in stocks because you do not achieve your objective 30 times, but you exceed your objective 40 times. Whereas, if

EXHIBIT 4-5

Asset Allocation 25-Year Distribution of Quarterly Returns (1971–1995)

Returns	100% S&P 500	60/40	40/60	100% T-Bond
−26 to −25	1	0	0	0
−25 to −24	0	0	0	0
−24 to −23	0	0	0	0
−23 to −22	1	0	0	0
−22 to −21	0	0	0	0
−21 to −20	0	0	0	0
−20 to −19	0	0	0	0
−19 to −18	0	0	0	0
−18 to −17	0	0	0	0
−17 to −16	0	0	0	0
−16 to −15	0	0	0	0
−15 to −14	0	0	0	1
−14 to −13	1	0	0	0
−13 to −12	0	0	0	0
−12 to −11	0	0	0	1
−11 to −10	2	1	2	0
−10 to −9	1	2	1	0
−9 to −8	0	1	0	1
−8 to −7	3	1	0	0
−7 to −6	1	0	1	1
−6 to −5	1	2	3	2
−5 to −4	5	3	1	4
−4 to −3	2	7	8	4
−3 to −2	6	3	6	4
−2 to −1	0	6	6	7
−1 to 0	6	2	4	11
Totals	**30**	**29**	**32**	**36**

Numbers of Quarters with Negative Returns

Returns	100% S&P 500	60/40	40/60	100% T-Bond
0 to 1	7	6	5	10
1 to 2	4	5	6	9
2 to 3	5	6	7	8
3 to 4	5	11	10	4
Totals	**21**	**28**	**28**	**31**

Numbers of Quarters with Returns between 0% and 4%

Returns	100% S&P 500	60/40	40/60	100% T-Bond
4 to 5	4	7	11	6
5 to 6	8	7	6	2
6 to 7	3	8	1	3
7 to 8	7	1	5	7
8 to 9	6	3	3	4
9 to 10	7	6	4	2
10 to 11	2	3	3	1
11 to 12	3	1	1	1
12 to 13	0	0	1	0
13 to 14	1	1	1	3
14 to 15	3	3	1	1
15 to 16	1	1	0	0
16 to 17	0	1	1	0
17 to 18	1	1	1	0
18 to 19	1	0	0	0
19 to 20	0	0	1	1
20 to 21	0	0	0	1
21 to 22	1	0	0	0
22 to 23	1	0	0	0
23 to 24	0	0	0	0
24 to 25	0	0	0	0
25 to 26	0	0	0	1
Totals	**49**	**43**	**40**	**33**

Numbers of Quarters with Returns Greater than 4%

you are 100 percent in bonds, you do not achieve your objective 36 times and you only do better 33 times. You have more downside periods in bonds without as much upside potential.

What happens if you mix your assets? In this case, 60 percent S&P and 40 percent bonds. You only have 29 losses and you have 43 winners.

What happens if you mix it 40–60? You get 32 losses and 40 winners. So you can see that if you want to minimize your risk, the best thing to do is have a 60% S&P: 40% bond ratio.

There are times we do not want to have this ratio. When stocks are at 24 or 26 times earnings, you may want to take 5 to 15 percent out of stocks and move it over to bonds. When P/E multiples go higher, you may want to take another 5 percent, and so on. What happens is that over time, you will move up and down this asset allocation curve. In other words, you buy bonds when they are cheap (high interest rates) and shift over to stocks when they are cheap (low PE multiples). Develop those weak hands into strong hands.

The cycles also help us know when more of your money should be in bonds and when you should have more of it in stocks.

We can do this by "buying" money management styles (private or mutual funds) that are consistent, then mix the allocation amounts, and mix investment styles between value and growth. The net result is that the three portfolios shown in Exhibit 4–6 (Heritage, Benchmark, and Pilot) made more money than the average mutual fund and beat the index.

It's that simple. Well, only if you stay through the entire cycle. As studies have shown, the average mutual fund investor manages to lose 2.2 percent, while the growth funds made 12.5 percent a year. (See Exhibit 4–7.)

EXHIBIT 4 – 6

Three Optimally Weighted Portfolios

★ Heritage Portfolio of Mutual Funds

Primary objective is to conserve principal by maintaining at all times a balanced portfolio of both stocks and bonds. Each mutual fund is optimally weighted within the portfolio to produce enhanced returns with reduced risk relative to peers and a balanced index. The Heritage Portfolio seeks both income and capital appreciation for a period of approximately five years in a portfolio comprised of six to eight superior mutual funds.

★ Benchmark Portfolio of Mutual Funds

The Benchmark Portfolio is an effective way to allocate mutual funds into a growth strategy that concentrates on those mutual funds that demonstrate a track record of superior returns relative to risk. Each mutual fund is optimally weighted by investment style and sector allocation to produce enhanced returns with reduced risk relative to a historical benchmark—the S&P 500 Index. The Benchmark Portfolio seeks capital appreciation for a period of approximately five years in a portfolio comprised of five to seven superior mutual funds.

★ Pilot Portfolio of Mutual Funds

Aims to obtain maximum capital appreciation in an optimally weighted portfolio that concentrates on those mutual funds that demonstrate a five-year track record of maximum returns relative to peers and historical benchmarks—Russell 2000 and S&P 500 Index. The Pilot Portfolio seeks aggressive capital appreciation for a period of five years in a portfolio comprised of five to seven superior mutual funds.

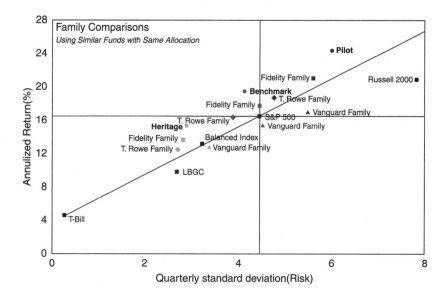

EXHIBIT 4 – 7

The Disparity Between Investment Returns and Investor's Return

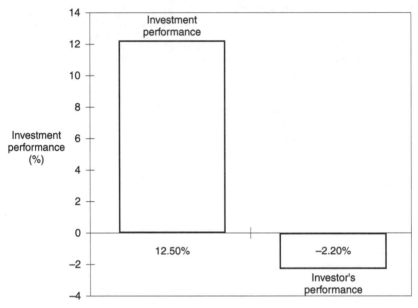

Source: Morningstar and AFA Financial. Reprinted with permission.

I spent a lot of time on the subject of mixing stocks and bonds to explain one thing: *Your best asset allocation mix is 60 percent S&P stocks and 40 percent bonds.* If you understand this one principle, you will do better than 70 percent of the "professional" investment managers. The bottom line is this: the more diversification, the less risk. Exhibit 4–8 clearly shows the benefits of diversification.

Diversification also allows you to select different investment vehicles—such as small-company stocks or international equities—which by themselves are volatile but as part of a mix generate less overall volatility, and provide the potential for greater return.

So you can have lower risk but still get higher returns through diversification of asset classes and investment styles. Recently this process has been called "strategic asset allocation."

Strategic asset allocation simply pinpoints the most efficient way to harness the benefits of diversification. Taking the diversification a step or two further than simply asset class diversification, it also includes investment style diversification (value versus growth), esoteric investment vehicle diversification, and lifestyle allocation.

> So you can have lower risk but still get higher returns through diversification of asset classes and investment styles.

Traditional wisdom has it that risk and return go hand in hand, always traveling in the same direction. Higher returns mean more risk; less risk equals lower returns. This is not really so. It is one of those pseudo-rules taught in basic investment books.

Without increasing your present level of volatility, for example, you may be able to increase returns simply by changing the way your portfolio is structured.

How much can you increase returns? Consider Exhibit 4–9, which shows the returns of portfolios allocated between Treasury bills and stocks (S&P 500) over a 25-year period.

So the answer is: a lot, if you take a long-term perspective. A 1 percent or 2 percent improvement may not seem like much in the short run. But even small increases, earned regularly and compounded over the years, make a big dollar difference in the long run.

And all because many money managers are using strategic asset allocation. It should start to become clear why the concept has become so "hot." The fact that some people are using the term as a marketing gimmick does not diminish its value. Strategic asset allocation is a step beyond traditional asset class diversification. But once the strategy has been

EXHIBIT 4–8

The Power of Diversification—as an Investment Strategy

The two bar charts on the left illustrate what would happen over 25 years if you invested $100,000 in an 8 percent fixed rate instrument. As you can see, the $100,000 grows to $684,850.

The following two bar charts illustrate the power of diversification. Imagine that you took the same $100,000 and equally invested it in five different vehicles that returned over 25 years as follows:

- You lost the first $20,000—not 20 percent or 50 percent—but actually lost it all!
- You broke even on the second $20,000—zero return!
- You earn 5 percent per year on the third $20,000

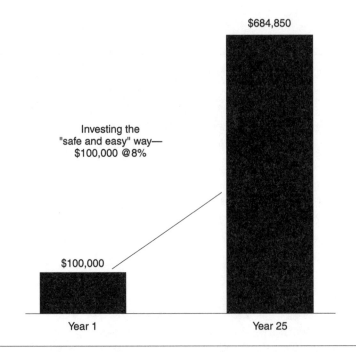

EXHIBIT 4-8 (CONT.)

The Power of Diversification—as an Investment Strategy

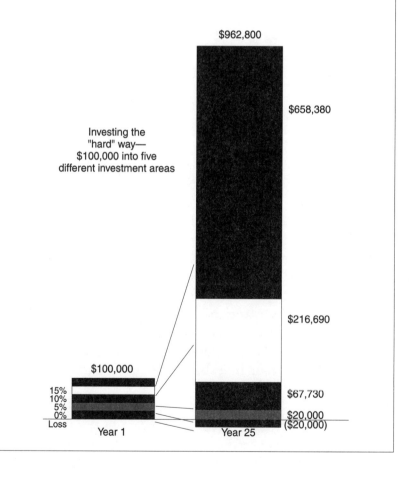

- You earn 10 percent per year on the fourth $20,000
- You earn 15 percent per year on the fifth $20,000

As you can see, even with the disparity in performance, the diversified strategy grew to $962,800, which is 40 percent higher or a full $277,950 more than the first example.

$962,800

$658,380

Investing the
"hard" way—
$100,000 into five
different investment areas

$216,690

$100,000

$67,730

15%	
10%	
5%	
0%	$20,000
Loss	($20,000)

Year 1   Year 25

EXHIBIT 4 – 9

Asset Allocation: 25-Year Annualized Returns & Growth
of a Dollar (1971–1995)

25-Year Period Ending 12-31-95

	Annualized Returns	Ending $ Value
T-Bond	9.64	$ 9.98
60% T-Bond/40% S&P 500	10.96	$13.47
40% T-Bond/60% S&P 500	11.46	$15.08
S&P 500	12.14	$17.53

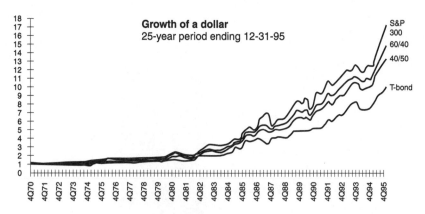

implemented, its tactical implementation is the key to keep
it working. Tilting to position your portfolio for what is ahead
in the business cycle is a critical part of the process.

In brief, asset or portfolio allocation extends the concept of
diversification by attempting to match specific models of
diversification to the objectives and risk tolerances of a particular individual. "Risk tolerances" mean the amount of risk
you can take in your investment program and still sleep at
night.

The 1987 market crash spurred interest in the development
of model portfolios based on this concept. It suddenly became
much easier to interest investors in an investment approach
that recognized market risks and personal tolerance for
those risks. (You will recall that before the crash, many

investors were being carried away with "the sky's the limit" mentality; greed in high gear.)

A landmark Ibbotson study[1] concluded that asset allocation accounted for 91.5 percent of the return, while only 4.6 percent was attributable to the selection of a particular stock, bond, or other investment, 1.8 percent attributed to market timing, and 2.1 percent to other factors. Exhibit 4–10 graphically illustrates this study.

EXHIBIT 4–10

Which, Where & How Much . . .

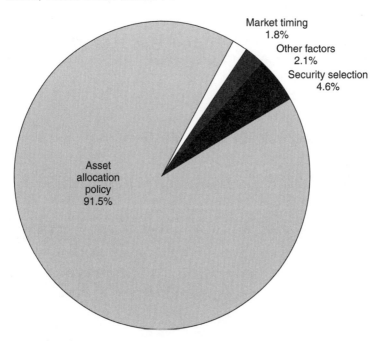

91.5% of portfolio return is from allocation

---

[1]*Asset Allocation Decision, 1990–1993,* (Chicago: Ibbotson Associates, 1994). Reprinted with permission.

The study found that 91.5 percent of investment return was a result of strategic asset allocation. The selection of a particular investment accounted for only 8.5 percent of the total return. I want to point this out to discourage you from buying individual stocks without regard to their tactical usefulness. Such nontactical investments eventually become scattered assets.

These studies indicate that paying more attention to how a portfolio is allocated will result in the greatest return. Put another way, the search for the one ideal stock is not the most productive way to increase your portfolio value.

To recap, diversification is a way of reducing investment risk. In fact, by investing in a variety of investments, the overall performance should be less volatile than if you put all your money in one type of investment, such as a single stock or bond. And strategic asset allocation ties it all together, giving you the best of all worlds.

ANOTHER CATEGORY OF RISK: EMOTIONAL RISK

Before we go on, I want to discuss one last advanced fundamental element, "emotional risk." Investment risks can be broken down into two broad categories: investment risk and emotional risk. Together, these two types of risk are typically the driving force behind your investment decision-making process.

The principles of financial risk—investment risk—are probably best understood by examining the past market results of different types of assets, which we have been doing throughout this discussion. What we have not discussed yet is emotional risk, and that is the one area that "Type A" decision makers most often neglect. When decision makers are too focused or reacting too quickly, they often forget to take their own emotions into account. To be a successful investment entrepreneur, you have to control your emotions and not let them enter into a decision.

Emotional risk is an intangible and sometimes costly form of risk. Investors who misjudge their ability to handle uncertainty often find themselves running out of patience with their investments at the worst possible times—at the top of

> Emotional risk is an intangible and sometimes costly form of risk.

bull markets and at the bottom of bear markets. For example, in bull markets, the emotional element sometimes causes investors to increase their holdings in stocks by selling the "underperforming" fixed-income portion of their portfolio, only to become overexposed in expensive stocks at market highs.

These same investors often do just the opposite in bear markets. They liquidate stocks that have declined in value precipitously and buy fixed-income securities at market lows. Then, when the stock market recovers, they are no longer positioned to take advantage of it. How many people were selling stock as the market plunged during the months leading up to the war in the Persian Gulf? Those who sold were acting on impulse, thinking that the stock market would continue to fall forever.

The last basic principle in this section on fundamentals of investing is, therefore, controlling your emotions. Take a step back and notice what emotion you're in when you are about to make an investment decision. And remember to check to see if you aren't reacting to the day's news headlines. Remember Tom Brokaw's comment to me—"if it bleeds, it leads." The media often play off of investors' fears, and furthermore, they are motivated by very short-term time horizons (one day) as opposed to the wise investor's long-term horizon. So if you're feeling nervous about your investment, stop to consider the state of the news for the day and then consider what the P/E multiples of the market are and where we are in the business cycle—two tools you now have from the discussion so far.

Another advantage such a review offers is that it can alert you to what I call "The Magic Moment," a scenario every investment entrepreneur uses for all it's worth. What is this "Magic Moment"? Read on . . .

5

The "Magic Moment"

There are a number of forces constantly at work in the stock market. Buying and selling pressure is motivated by the current stage of the business cycle. Value is created by the market price relative to buying and selling pressure and earnings. What happens if earnings stop going up in a recession and actually decline? Stock prices start coming down. But if earnings go up in a stagnation period or recession, the earning increase can support the price of the stock; we can have a "silent crash" as in 1991–94. It was a silent crash because it didn't make the headlines; the media doesn't understand it and therefore they don't report it. Your next step is to understand a silent crash and learn how to recognize and take advantage of it.

SILENT CRASH

If the Dow is at 3,000 and those select companies are earning
$500 a share, then the Dow is at six times earnings (3,000
divided by 500 = 6). If the Dow stays at 3,000 and we go into
a recession and the market does not go down but the earnings drop to $400 a share, we are now at 7.5 times earnings
(3,000 divided by 400 = 7.5). If earnings drop to $300 a share,
we are at 10 times earnings. Now you get an idea why P/E is
a fundamental tool.

These two variables, price and earnings, are constantly
working against each other, and are rarely reported by newscasters or salesmen. As we showed in Chapter 2, you can
accurately measure price/earnings multiples and determine
the true value of the stock market. If your goal is to double
the market, you must really understand what a P/E multiple
is and how it relates to business cycle in order to use this
entrepreneurial tool.

We touched on this in our introduction discussion of how the
market is valued in Chapter 2. Let's take a closer look so
you'll really be an expert at it and know when and how to
make your moves.

If we look at the period between 1952 and 1994, we find that
the stock market has generally traded on the low end of the
price/earnings multiple of about 10 times earnings and a
high end of around 26 times earnings. How much is the
investing public willing to discount future earnings to pay
for a company today? In robust times, the heady public is
willing to invest in a company and wait 20 or 30 years for
the payback. "Wall Street" says, "thank you," and sells you
stock and invents new stocks to satisfy insatiable demand.
These are called "IPOs," initial public offerings. In negative
times, the same investor will sell that stock to someone else

for a 10-year payback. "Wall Street" says, "thank you," and buys your stock (fear) for Wall Street inventory. We call this "weak hands giving to strong hands." One can see that measuring the market in P/E multiples of 10 to 26 is about the normal range. The median is at 14–16 times earnings. (Refer back to Exhibit 2–15 for a recap of this concept.)

Because most of the public has no understanding of market value (P/E), it is believed by many that 1,000, 2,000, 3,000, 4,000, and 5,000 point marks are milestones. Why? A market at 4,000 trading at 14 times earnings is a lot cheaper than a market at 3,000 trading at 25 times earnings. Yet most investors think improperly that 4,000 is a valid measure. The public also thinks that an increase of 1,000 points in the Dow average is a big move. No, not always.The increase from 1,000 to 2,000 was a 100 percent increase. The 1995 move from 4,000 to 5,000, while 1,000 points, was only a 25 percent increase—a big difference. The move from 5,000 to 10,000 is also 100 percent. If the market increases 15 percent a year, we will see 10,000 by the year 2000. Get it?

> The public also thinks that an increase of 1,000 points in the Dow average is a big move. No, not always.

Unfortunately, the public does not realize that this myth is perpetuated by "headline writers" whose job it is to get people's attention and sell newspapers. In January 1994, people started selling their stocks because the DJIA was "high" at 3,832. But it wasn't high! The Dow actually was as cheap as it had been at any time since World War II. By the end of 1995, the Dow was at 15.5 times earnings, and it was at the lower end of the range since the beginning of the post-war economy. Next pause, 6,400? By 2010, it will be 20,000. Believe it!

Price/Earnings Valuation

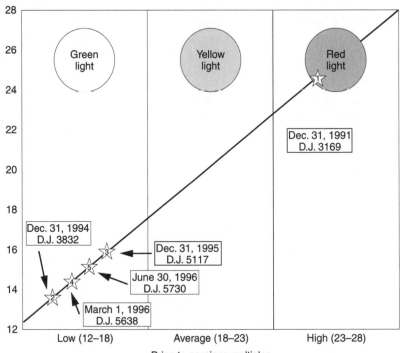

Price to earnings multiples

Exhibit 5–1 (which repeats Exhibit 2–16) puts some hard numbers to this. It shows the overall market P/E level at various dates during recent years. The first star from the right (December 31, 1991) shows the DJIA at 3,169 when the P/E was approximately 25—a high market.

Follow the line down to #2 (December 31, 1994), which shows the market at the end of the "silent crash." Even though the market was at 3,832, the P/E was under 14—a cheap market. Even 18 months later (#5, June 30, 1996) the P/E was still cheap at about 15.

Dan or Connie, or Walter before them, all probably know less about the stock market than you do, and are given—every day, free of charge—the Dow Jones as news to report. Dow Jones' point values are broadcast daily by the news without any explanation of their impact, for example, "The market was up big today, a record move of 150 points." Well, at a 3,000 Dow that is big: 150 divided by 3,000 = 5 percent. If the Dow is at 5,000, that 150-point move is 150 divided by 5,000 = 2.5 percent.

The public has been trained to look to the Dow Jones (only 30 industrial stocks) for guidance. They have been trained in headline mathematics. Every time you get to a multiple or a decile—10, 20, 30, 100, 1,000—you have been trained to think it is a new milestone. "I can't wait until I accumulate $1,000." "Homes have just broken the $100,000 level." "I wish I had a million dollars." All of our training is in round numbers.

Think back to what happened when the Dow Jones hit 1,000. What did the newspapers report? "Dow Jones Reaches New High." "The Market Made It." "Countdown to New Highs." Investment advisors were interviewed and 40 percent advised to bail out; the market was too high. And what happened? John and Jane Q. Public responded: "You never go broke taking a profit. I'd better sell now while the market's at a brand new high."

Traders on Wall Street were rubbing their hands together. They knew that the "Monster" was inciting the public to sell. The public was going to sell because of an all-new "high." How did the public know "it's an all-new high?" Because the press was reporting "the facts"; it must be true if it's in print. The public rushed in like bulls and Wall Street responded like matadors. "Wall Street"

> Traders on Wall Street were rubbing their hands together. They knew that the "Monster" was inciting the public to sell.

institutional investors came to investment advisors such as myself wanting to buy IBM at, say, $50 a share. Now look at what happens in such a case. "Wall Street" knows the impact of fear and uncertainty; it will even wave a red flag by commenting that Merrill, Dean, Salomon, Bear—the major brokerage firms and therefore the experts—question the value of IBM and the stock market. Some of the research analysts may even put out negative opinions. So John and Jane Q. Public, the "bull," come raging in. They are looking at "Wall Street." They have 100 shares of IBM to sell at $80—the price yesterday. What does "Wall Street" do? They do not buy. They step aside as the market dies. The stock goes down from $80 to $70 to $60 to $50, down to $45. Then it looks good to "Wall Street," so "The Street" steps in and buys for their own account.

"Wall Street" then makes a report, "Market Looks Cheap at This Point—"Earnings on IBM Expected to Go Higher." The press headlines ask, "Will the Market Make It This Time?" "Is This the Start of a New Bear Market?" So, IBM rallies to $70. Investors say, "Oh, it's back near where it was; maybe I'd better sell." They start selling and what happens? The price goes down again. When it hits $50, Wall Street buys because it thinks that is a cheap price. Up and down, how many times? Three times, four times. The headlines, "75 Percent of Investment Managers Are Bears at This Time." "Public Confidence Is Shaken." "O.J. Simpson Trial May Impact Consumer Confidence." Then what? Look at January 1995. When sellers were exhausted and the money was transferred from weak hands to strong hands, the market exploded. Why? Not because it broke 4,000, but because P/E multiples were cheap—too cheap—14 times earnings.

What happens when the market hits 6,000, 7,000, 10,000? It will be the same thing all over again. Yes, the Monster awaits—the magic moment. It waits for your stock—your fear and greed!

If the Dow were indicative of value, why did the stock market crash in 1987? The index "value" had nothing to do with it. At 2,700 in August of 1987, the P/E multiple was at 26 times earnings. That is when the institutions started selling. That is why the market came down. It bottomed out at around 16 times earnings October 19. The market repeated the process three times.

That is what I look for—the **"magic moment."** This is when the P/E hits its bottom band of 10–14 and it gives you an excellent opportunity to buy at cyclical lows.

The stock market had, from 1991–94, been unable to break 4,000 because of the following legitimate concerns. The market was at 22–24 times earnings in December 1991. But guess what has happened between 1991 and 1994? The market had become 40 percent cheaper because it dropped to 14 times earnings. How many times will John and Jane Q. Public fall for this? Forever; yes, forever. Except you now know what to do at these magic moments. You know what to look for. So learn to automatically translate the day's stock market movements into the corresponding P/E, and in particular, be on the lookout for when the P/E approaches lower than 16. This signals an approaching magic moment and you want to reap the benefits it offers.

Exhibit 5–1 illustrates three of my rules. The "Green Light" is when conditions make stock ownership relatively safe. The "Yellow Light" is normal market conditions—use caution. And the "Red Light" is when there are high P/E multiples— look out!

TWO

BECOME AN EXPERT AT MONEY MANAGER SELECTION

Now that you know the market fundamentals plus a few other tools, you're way ahead of most investors.

But you're also a very busy person. I know this from the many clients I've worked with over the years. Finding the time to actively manage both your business and your investments can seem impossible, and while you've now got the basics of investing down, a successful investment program requires a lot of time and painstaking effort.

If what you learned in Part One unleashed a burning passion for investment, by all means go with it. But because your assets are vital not only to you but to your business as well, I recommend that you leave the actual management to a professional money manager.

So, you ask, why all the preliminary information on knowing the market? Because just as your mechanic "respects" you more when it's obvious you know the basics of what's going on with your car, so does your money manager or broker when he knows you know the business. This is a highly competitive field and the manager has to work to keep you—and harder when you know the basics of what he's doing.

Then, too, the fundamentals you learned in Part One are useful in figuring out which managers to select, because, believe me, there are a lot of them out there. In Part Two, you'll learn the ins and outs of manager selection and how to spot those who'd like to pull the wool over your eyes. Read on.

6

The Statement of Investment Expectations

One of the most important management tools in a successful investment program is the statement of investment expectations. It is the foundation upon which investment goals, manager evaluation, and monitoring should be based. I use this tool with my clients for two main reasons. One, it helps them focus on their goals and two, it outlines how to get to those goals. For you this means that you will select appropriate investment managers for your investment program because your guidelines are in place.

The statement of investment objectives should be in the form of a clear and specific written working document. Broad-based generalities do not serve well as investment objectives. Being specific is the key to providing a proper working investment plan. "Long-term appreciation" is a nebulous goal. A better example might be average growth of inflation plus 5 percent during rolling five-year periods, or 1 percent more than the S&P 500 for a rolling five-year period. Qualitative aspects are also important. Therefore, at a minimum, the following items should be covered when designing an investment policy statement:

1. The investment objective, using nominal return benchmarks, with consideration of the "relative" rate of return, that is, 1 percent above the S&P 500, or 1 percent above the median value manager, and so on. *Example:* The investment objective is to produce a total return, net of expenses, that will surpass the market index, on average, for full-market cycles by 10 percent. So, if the S&P 500 is up 15 percent per year, the portfolio should produce 16.5 percent net.

2. Definitions of "risk."

3. Risk tolerance. *Example:* Investment risk—for value accounts I am willing to accept a portfolio that is down as much as 5 percent in any given year; for growth accounts, 10 percent.

4. Time period for review and evaluation.

5. Allowable investments and quality standards.

6. Liquidity requirements.

7. Policy asset allocation. *Example:* I will always have at least 40 percent in value or growth but no more than 60 percent in one or the other. I can put 20 percent in the money market.

8. Procedure for selecting and dismissing money managers.

9. Cash flow of the plan (both in and out).

When you have more than one manager, create this overall statement for yourself for all the portfolios, and then create individual statements for each manager to follow. Keep copies of the individual manager statements with your over-all statement for easy reference and review purposes.

The written investment plan objectives do not have to be overly complex as long as they are specific and closely state your needs and goals. Some very comprehensive plans have been contained in one page.

Remember, your investment managers will expect you to follow the plan. If they are achieving your plan, you should not replace them if they are at a low spot in the cycle.

The portfolio's assets are to be managed and invested with the objective of achieving the greatest return consistent with the level of liquidity and risk sufficient to meet your financial needs.

> The portfolio's assets are to be managed and invested with the objective of achieving the greatest return consistent with the level of liquidity and risk sufficient to meet your financial needs.

ADDITIONAL EXAMPLES OF INVESTMENT GUIDELINES

1. Common stocks have a place in my investment portfolio; also bonds should be included in this portfolio for adequate diversification. Generally, bonds should never exceed 50 percent of the portfolio at any time and stocks should never exceed 80 percent of the portfolio at any one time.
2. There will be at least two equity portfolios, one value and the other growth. My bonds will be managed by (myself or name of manager).
3. My investment philosophy is that each portfolio manager should invest broadly in stocks that are consid-

ered to have potential to exceed the S&P 500 and the style indexes, and that the portfolio manager will generally sell individual stocks when they no longer are considered appropriate for my objective.

4. My portfolio is balanced with emphasis on total return, which is capital growth plus income. I view risk both as long-term erosion of capital (inflation), plus the possibility of a negative performance in the value of the portfolio when compared to its appropriate index (i.e., S&P 500, value peer group, etc.).

5. I expect my portfolio to have similar fluctuations as the market index or the style index.

The following are acceptable asset classes:

- Common stocks
- Convertible bonds (treated as equity)
- U.S. government securities
- Corporate bonds—with no rating below A
- Commercial paper
- Money market funds/Treasury bills

6. Investments should be chosen from the NYSE, ASE, regional exchanges, and the NASDAQ market. All assets must have readily ascertainable market value and be easily marketable.

The following are prohibited transactions or assets:

- Commodity trading, including all futures contracts
- Purchasing of letter stock
- Short selling
- Option trading
- Foreign securities

All institutional and pension fund investors use this type of statement of investment expectations; your assets are just as valuable and deserve one, too. As with any business plan, the

Statement of Investment Expectations keeps you focused and on track, key traits for success in business—and in investment. Once you have your Statement of Investment Expectations in hand you're ready to proceed in your search for the appropriate money managers for your plan.

Don't overlook this statement—it is the foundation of your strategy.

Recently, a neighbor and client—who was a very successful businessman—lost sight of his objective statement and began an uncomfortable financial journey. This individual had never been successful in the market but had made millions in his business. Prior to working with me, he had purchased IPOs in one-half-million-dollar lots and lost the majority of each investment. After listening to his tale of woe, I began my process with him. After beating the market by a factor of two or three years, and experiencing a 74 percent return in 1995, he thought investing was easy. He began market timing, believing he had acquired a magic touch. He moved substantial sums to a hedge fund where the hedge manager would get 22 percent of the profits. (By the way, the hedge fund had a six-month track record.) He also shipped his allocations to the manager who did best last quarter—then best last month—then best last week. I sent him on his way as he became more and more irrational about his abilities. He is clearly heading into "the soup" that you will learn about in Chapter 9. The lesson: Don't confuse brains with bull markets.

> **Don't confuse brains with bull markets.**

7 CHAPTER

Selecting Money Managers: Part One— Paring the Pool

I categorize my private money managers by their investment styles, that is, whether they are growth or value managers. As we have seen, a particular investment style will work during a certain market cycle. If we understand where the economy is in a business cycle, then we can anticipate where the market should be or is headed. But there is still a problem. No one knows for sure what the market will do. We have a better sense of what the business cycle will do; unfortunately, we don't know when. So just as we diversify our assets, we must hedge our bets by having several managers with completely different investment styles.

These different investment styles must be zigzagging with a positive correlation. But if I have a zig manager and combine that manager with a zag manager, what do I have? A performance that is balanced right down the middle—a portfolio with reduced volatility.

Since approximately 70 percent of mutual funds and most managers do not even perform as well as the market, I do not even waste my time by looking at the managers of that 70 percent. I study the 30 percent who do better than the market. I put all of these mutual funds and private money managers into my evaluation system and I track them according to "adherence." I throw out any manager who is not doing as well as the market over a complete cycle.

THE SORTING PROCESS

I take the remaining managers and put them all into a sorting process. The first thing I want to categorize is investment style. Is this or that particular manager aggressive or conservative? In other words, is this one a growth manager, a value manager, or some combination of the two, for example, sector rotation. Then what size stocks do they invest in—big, medium, or small?

I then use a systematic process to come up with a pool of select managers for each style. I take each growth manager and compare "it" to the group of growth managers as a whole. I look for all growth managers who beat (1) the S&P 500; (2) the growth manager peer group index; (3) the growth stock index; and (4) their capitalization category—small, medium, or large cap—over the market cycle. I throw out quite a few managers, about 70 percent of this 30 percent, because most managers do not keep up. I'm left with about 10 percent of all growth managers to study.

I do the same thing with value managers. I am going to throw out all the value managers who did not beat the S&P 500, and the value managers' peer group index, the value stock median, and their capitalization group. Same results;

about 10 percent are left. This same process is used in my review of mutual funds as well as private portfolio investment managers.

By using this process, I pare down the list of managers from a universe of 22,000 to about 2,000. Then I eliminate those who are not managing $100 million or more. In order for a manager to have enough revenue to buy the research he needs, we know "he" has to manage more than $100 million. Even $100 million isn't much anymore. A typical fee of 1 percent hardly begins to pay for staff, research, travel, marketing, and so on.

America's most popular mutual funds are right here, producing average returns and sometimes taking above-average risk. (See Exhibit 7–1.)

The reason these funds are the most popular is that they have the most money. The reason they have the most money is that they have the biggest advertising budget and advertising people often do not worry about the whole truth—just include enough to get by the regulators.

I utilize all the criteria that have been discussed and look for managers whom I find are consistent and reliable. Then I choose the most consistent universe of managers from the list and apply the risk/return analysis to search for low volatility. The current list is provided later in this book.

Independent Investment Management Firms

My favorite—why? Because they provide the most flexible and complete array of personalized investment services for the private client or the intermediate-sized pension sponsor, and when times are tough, you can talk directly to the portfolio manager.

EXHIBIT 7–1

5-Year Risk/Return Analysis for Period Ending 2Q96

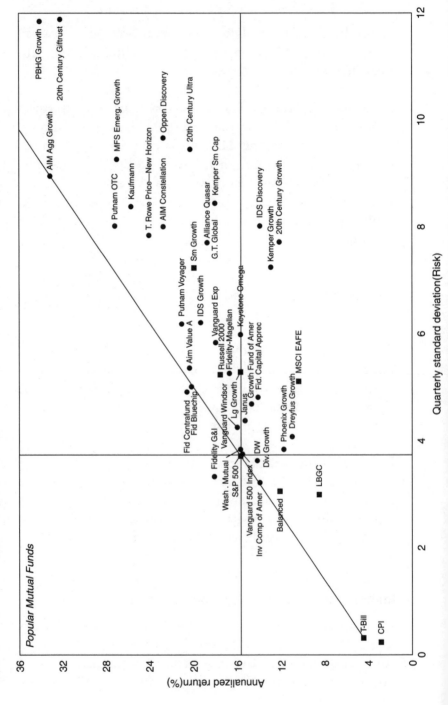

Popular Mutual Funds

- They are usually owned by investment professionals who offer individual account management. The highly competitive field of independent investment management coupled with potentially huge financial results encourages these professionals to strive for superior performance.
- These professionals are frequently well compensated— such firms experience a minimum of personnel turnover.
- Any broker with any firm, and any professional investment consultant, can refer you to them.
- You are not locked into any one method of distribution nor are you charged a front-end or back-end commission.

Back in the mid-70s, there were 2,500 independent money managers; at present, they're approaching 22,000 and the number is quickly growing. Banks, insurance companies, mutual funds, and brokerage firms have all been spawning grounds for independent talent. Those who go out on their own as independent money managers are frequently the "best of the best."

It is to the independent money manager's credit that his entrepreneurial spirit has taken him out of the corporate structure and encouraged him to strike out on his own, where the code is "survival of the fittest."

Many investment management companies are operated as a partnership. On an individual basis, each portfolio manager or research analyst is evaluated by the investment management firm to ascertain his or her qualifications and overall compatibility. This assures continuity of philosophy.

Banks have begun to recognize the expertise of the independent money manager. Some banks have even closed down their money management departments, realizing they are not doing the most efficient job. Some have subcontracted to independent investment managers, while others resort to "peddling" their own brand of mutual fund, a bank logo, and a hired "sub-adviser."

Independent money managers, in my opinion, are the epitome of the capitalist system that fosters development of wealth. Highly motivated by the capitalistic system, they tend to do well for their clients and themselves. That is not to say that every money manager is better than every brokerage firm or mutual fund, for that is hardly the case.

Success still depends, however, on choosing the money manager whose investment style most effectively complements your investment objectives and goals.

8

Don't Jump on the Indexing Bandwagon!

I have heard so much about passive investing. Why can't I just buy an index mutual fund and not worry about trying to beat the market?"

Before proceeding further, I want to address this question. It's not new to me. In fact, I often hear it because investors assume it's an effective and easy way to invest. Passive, or index, investing is basically setting up a portfolio to match the contents of a particular index. It's a strategy that has become popular in recent years, but as I'll explain, it's not a good idea for the entrepreneurial investor who wants to double his money simply because it is passive and doesn't always work with the business cycle.

Let me explain how the large pension plans were drawn into the indexing game during the late 1980s. The thinking then was that if 80 percent of money managers underperformed the market, it seemed logical to simply invest with the benchmark or an index fund representing the stock market.

But here is the rub. This thinking preceded the basic fundamental style analysis. Many investors failed to recognize that these 80 percent were lower-risk managers who probably carried cash or had an investment style dealing with a certain sector of the market. Those with other investment styles were starting to produce better results than the S&P 500.

Also, during that time, there was a most unusual stock market with falling inflation rates combined with rising corporate profits, mergers, and acquisitions. It was an ideal investment environment for indexing. It is not surprising that indexing became popular by 1991, the last big move up in large cap stocks.

By indexing, one could own stock in large, well-known companies. These were the very companies that profited most from the leveraged buyouts and takeovers that proliferated in the markets of the '80s.

But today, we are in a different economic environment. We are seeing slow growth, low interest rates, and low inflation. Index investors will be in for a disappointment. Investors and pension funds are not going to achieve the 17.5 percent returns that indexing gave them in the 1980s.

> We are seeing slow growth, low interest rates, and low inflation.

During the 1980s, particularly from 1982 to 1987, being fully invested in the top 100 stocks was clearly the thing to do because those stocks were so undervalued. In fact, being out

EXHIBIT 8-1

Missing a Few Good Days Substantially Reduces Return

1980–1989	S&P 500 Annualized Return*
All 2,528 trading days:	17.50%
Minus 10 best days:	12.60%
Minus 20 best days:	9.30%
Minus 30 best days:	6.50%
Minus 40 best days:	3.90%

*Figures assume that when not invested in stocks, assets were earning interest at the average rate of 30-day Treasury bills over the 1980–1989 period.

of the index only 40 of the best days during the period of 1980 to 1989 reduced returns from 17.5 percent to 3.9 percent—a 13.6 percent per year difference. (See Exhibit 8–1.)

Big cap stocks took off and the small- and medium-cap sector, which had a rally in August 1983, went into its own bear market. This meant that if you were not fully invested, especially during that five-year period (1982 to 1987), you underperformed the market.

Since many managers consistently underperformed the S&P 500, for that period, that made a strong argument for owning an index fund. But those who gravitated toward indexing failed to recognize that they were not just moving away from money managers; they were buying into one investment style. That style was to own the "nifty 100." However, if you follow that style today, you are going to miss the next trend. That style worked well in the past but it does not appear to be working any more. This is why I emphasized the importance of knowing the stages of the business cycle in Chapter 2 and the growth and value investing cycles in Chapter 3. Look at Exhibit 8–2, which examines each year from 1987 to 1995. Five of the nine years, the S&P 500 underperformed the median investment advisor. Four of the nine years the S&P 500 was in the top 50 percent, but not once in any year was the S&P 500 in the top 25 percent.

EXHIBIT 8 – 2

So! Index Funds?
Equity Universe Performance Comparison for Period Ending 4Q95

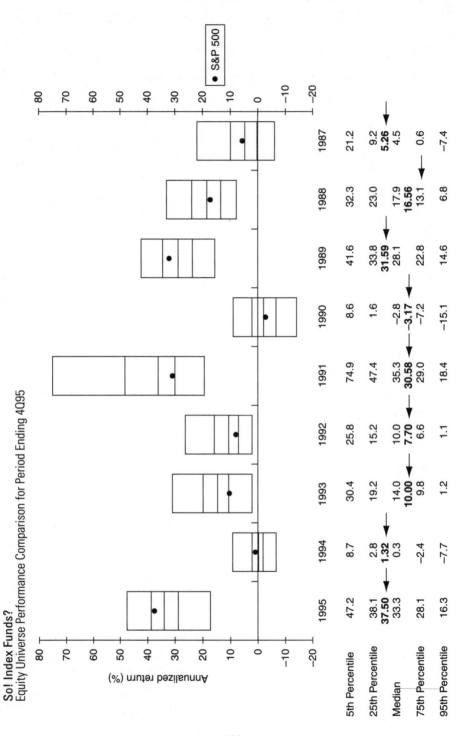

	1995	1994	1993	1992	1991	1990	1989	1988	1987
5th Percentile	47.2	8.7	30.4	25.8	74.9	8.6	41.6	32.3	21.2
25th Percentile	38.1	2.8	19.2	15.2	47.4	1.6	33.8	23.0	9.2
	37.50	**1.32**					**31.59**	17.9	**5.26**
Median	33.3	0.3	14.0	10.0	35.3	–2.8	28.1	**16.56**	4.5
			10.00	**7.70**	**30.58**	**–3.17**		13.1	
75th Percentile	28.1	–2.4	9.8	6.6	29.0	–7.2	22.8	6.8	0.6
95th Percentile	16.3	–7.7	1.2	1.1	18.4	–15.1	14.6		–7.4

100

In this decade, value-added will come by identifying those industries and companies that can operate in this new economic environment. It is an atmosphere that has very little pricing flexibility and little demand coming from the consumer. Why?

Because consumer goods make up two-thirds of the GNP. The average market indexes, however, don't have the same degree of representation of consumer goods companies. This new investment environment will make it almost impossible to achieve the same above-average returns by simply "blind" indexing.

Today, the consumer and many companies are still saddled with enormous debt. That's why consumer demand is not going up as it has in other recoveries. Today's consumers are too busy paying off their personal debts.

> Today, the consumer and many companies are still saddled with enormous debt. That's why consumer demand is not going up as it has in other recoveries.

As we approach the 21st century, we will see a somewhat sluggish worldwide growth. Few companies can thrive or even survive in this type of environment. This is where a good manager with a back-to-the-basics philosophy, using fundamental research in stock selection, can add value to a portfolio.

Pension plan managers will find it increasingly difficult to simply rely on the S&P to provide high returns. Historically, as we've seen, stocks compound at about 10 percent--not 17.5 percent as was experienced with index funds during the 1980s. Everyone wants to beat the averages, but with low volatility. The problem is that you can't have both unless you follow my disciplines.

Index funds have 100 percent market risk 100 percent of the time. Just as money came out of CDs and GICs (guaranteed income contracts) to be placed into bond funds—right at the peak, the same mistake will be made by jumping into index funds. Once everyone is involved in the same process, there is no longer value added. As with any trend, once discovered, it's time to look for the next one. You will soon learn about capture ratio—a tool that helps you find and track value-added investment managers.

Making the mistake of following conventional Wall Street wisdom is seldom the right strategy. It rarely pays off in the long run. The reality is that those heady days are done. Now our "rolling recession" economy favors companies that fill niches, that are lean and mean, flexible, and fast on their corporate feet.

> Making the mistake of following conventional Wall Street wisdom is seldom the right strategy.

In 1992, 1993, and 1994, a remarkably high percent of mutual funds outperformed index funds. I expect this trend to continue for years to come. Index funds are simply not selective enough. Today, there are twice as many mutual funds as there are stocks on the New York Stock Exchange.

1995 was a unique year that caught many mutual funds with a portion of their portfolio in cash. This was correct during the fourth quarter of 1994 (Orange County and Mexico), but two events occurred in January of 1995 that ended the competition before the race got through the first month. The California Public Employees Retirement Fund switched their asset allocation from 70 percent bonds to 70 percent stock almost overnight. The sheer power of investing tens of billions of dollars in stocks moved the S&P up almost 5 percent. During the second week, Greenspan indicated he would not anticipate a further increase in interest rates.

The market shot up another 5 percent. By the end of January 1995 the S&P 500 was already up almost 10 percent and most managers had cash reserves of up to 30 percent. The best they could do was scramble to catch the index.

The theme for the 1990s will probably encompass globalization, financial and retail sector restructuring, cyclical growth companies with strong franchises, health care, and environment cleanup. You want to be able to capitalize on these themes; indexing won't do that for you.

Now that we've covered this, let's get back to selecting the appropriate money managers.

9

CHAPTER

Selecting Money Managers: Part Two— Using the Risk/Reward Comparison

Remember the risk/reward chart we introduced in Chapter 3? Well, this is where it gets put into very useful practice. Exhibit 9–1 shows a risk/reward chart. Our goal is to get into the Northwest Quadrant of low risk, high returns.

Every one of us secretly believes we are entitled to high returns with little or no risk. We harbor that internal belief, and it is difficult to accept that we rarely achieve this ideal. Instead of performing high in the Northwest Quadrant, where we believe we're entitled to be, we're stuck in the Southeast Quadrant, the quadrant I call "the soup." Investments unfortunately often end up in "the soup."

To construct your own graph, or risk/return matrix, you need at least 12 to 20 quarters (or three to five years) of historical performance data. It's best to conduct the study over a full market cycle and then the most recent 1/2 cycle.

Study the illustration; recall that the matrix plots annualized return versus the volatility of the portfolio. Standard deviation (which we discussed in Chapter 3), measures the absolute volatility of each quarterly return around a certain mean return. The vertical axis measures the portfolio's return and the horizontal axis measures risk.

After plotting the returns on the matrix from Treasury bills and the stock market, draw a line connecting the two. That line is the capital return expectation line, a theoretical line representing investments without market risk (T-bills) and investments with inherent market risk (S&P 500 stocks). If investors assume more risk, they should be rewarded with a higher rate of return. That's why the capital market line slopes upward.

Anything above this line is in the "zone of efficiency." Anything beneath that line is in the "zone of inefficiency." Anything above the diagonal line is giving us what we believe we're entitled to—more return than the risk we are taking to achieve that return. So, why do we so often end up in "the soup"? (See Exhibit 9–1.)

Let's examine why. We have been trained to look to the past. Every year, the typical investors invest in last year's best mutual funds. Every year, investors invest in last year's best stock. Why? Because they believe past performance is an indicator of future performance. There is some merit in that; the problem comes with not looking at other relevant factors. It's like trying to drive down the super-highway looking only in the rear-view mirror. You would be making decisions based solely on where you've been, without considering what's ahead.

EXHIBIT 9–1

Historical Ranges of Returns and Risk for Various Investment Strategies
(1926–1995)

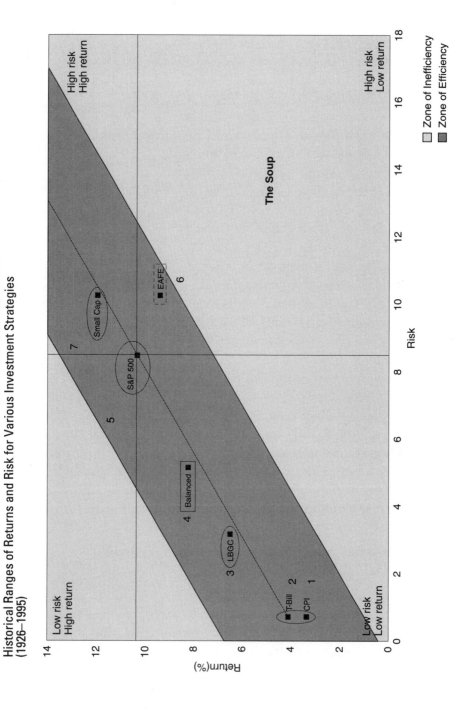

You're going to double the market by learning how to make decisions based not only on where you've been, but also on where you are and where you're going. That is the advantage of understanding the business cycle. In every business cycle, there are investment managers who are positioned to ascend into the Northwest Quadrant. The reason many investors end up in "the soup" is that they buy a product or select a manager already enjoying the efficiency zone without realizing that the business cycle is already beginning to force that product or manager out of the zone.

> You're going to double the market by learning how to make decisions based not only on where you've been, but also on where you are and where you're going.

Let's look into the true value of this zone of efficiency to see how we too can enjoy the ride on the upside, instead of simply buying last year's best performance. Our number one task is to find managers capable of achieving the efficiency zone at all. Reality is such, however, that over time every such manager is going to fall in and out of the optimum zone of efficiency. Our first job is to search for managers who have been both in and out of that zone of efficiency, and to predict which ones are likely to ascend again.

WHERE CAN YOU GET INFORMATION TO EVALUATE MANAGERS YOURSELF?

Every manager has this information available. Sometimes managers don't want to share it with you so you have to specifically ask for it: "I'd like to see your risk and return compared to other similar style investment managers." And the fact that you do lets them know you're an informed investor. But be very careful of the information provided by managers; it's such a tricky business I've devoted the entire next chapter to it. Avail yourself of information from independent money manager analysts such as Russel, Ibbotson, Nelsons Directory, Morning Star, Mobius, and of course, my company.

Managers are going to go in and out of peak performance, so another of our basic tools in doubling the market is to diversify among managers who are most often in the efficiency zone yet have different management styles.

Finally, we conduct capture ratio analysis, one of the last tools used in evaluating an investment manager. A northwest position in the *capture ratio* indicates the investment manager did not give back in declines as much as it made during rising periods. Exhibit 9–2 shows capture ratios of investment managers kept in a current portfolio.

The *capture ratio* measures the manager's return over a full market cycle and compares it to the relative index or benchmark. This *capture ratio* chart reflects several investment managers.

A graphic analysis of *capture ratio* is useful for comparing managers. Such charts look similar to a risk/return scatter diagram that describes return versus standard deviation. With *capture ratio,* however, the vertical axis is the upside capture ratio and the horizontal axis is the downside capture ratio. The higher the manager is on the vertical scale, the more return the manager has achieved. Ideally, the manager's portfolio has appreciated as much as the relative index. On the horizontal scale, the further the manager moves to the right, the more the manager declines with the market.

This is what is measures:

Investment manager

S&P 500

A manager's ability to resist decline in value.

EXHIBIT 9–2

Capture Ratio (versus Benchmark) for 5-Year Period

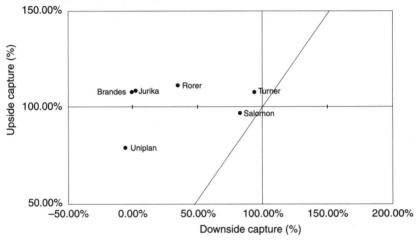

Manager composites prior to inception date

	# of Up Qtrs	Best Qtr	Upside Capture %	# of Down Qtrs	Worst Qtr	Downside Capture %
Salomon	15	6.7	96.76%	5	−2.7	82.61%
LBGC	15	6.5	100.00%	5	−3.2	100.00%
Uniplan	19	5.8	78.57%	1	−3.2	−6.26%
Bal Index	17	8.0	100.00%	3	−3.5	100.00%
Jurika	16	11.1	108.01%	4	−3.2	1.22%
Rorer	16	11.9	111.25%	4	−3.4	36.49%
Turner	15	13.3	107.52%	5	−4.3	94.20%
Brandes	14	11.7	107.86%	6	−4.0	−0.61%
S&P 500	16	9.7	100.00%	4	−3.8	100.00%

The crossmark on the graph is at 100 percent; this could easily be looked at as 100 points. If a manager plots above the vertical line, that manager has achieved more upside return than the index being compared. This would suggest that, as with scatter diagrams, the "northwest" quadrant is the most desirable place to find a manager whereas the "southeast" quadrant is the least desirable. The diagonal line represents all points for which the upside capture ratio is equal to the downside capture ratio. If a manager plots above the diagonal, that manager has achieved more upside than downside capture. As with the capital market line in risk/return scatter diagrams, it is more desirable to fall above the diagonal than below it.

From the *capture ratio* chart above, clearly money managers Brandes, Jurika, and Rorer have achieved superior results. Also, note that a negative downside capture ratio indicates the manager not only provided a cushion during a market decline, but produced a positive return during that same period. For example, the S&P 500 experienced four down quarters for the five-year period ending March 31, 1996, while Brandes was up 0.61 percent during the same period. In this downside study, a minus (–) indicates positive returns.

So now we know how to evaluate all the many money managers to see who best fits your requirements. Before going further, however, let's take a slight step back and look at what exactly those performance numbers are telling us, because yes, it's true, performance numbers can get confusing and they are only part of the process.

10

How Performance Can Get Confusing

There is a lot of confusion about investment performance. It seems that each mutual fund or investment manager claims it is number one in the country. How can this be? Everyone cannot be number one! There are many things in the investment industry that will get in your way and cloud your vision if you're not on the alert for them.

The typical mutual fund's advertising department picks the optimum time period performance to display in financial magazines. There will be some period when a mutual fund or money manager will show top performance. This is called Time Series Lie.

Mutual funds, banks, brokers, insurance companies, and money managers use a variety of methods to calculate investment returns. While the different approaches are usually perfectly legitimate, they can make comparison difficult.

One thing to keep in mind: Performance figures in brochures are there for one reason—marketing.

You can solicit help in deciphering performance figures from a knowledgeable broker, investment management consultant, or financial advisor or you can take the time to gain a better understanding of how performance is reported and how risk-and-return statistics work. In these ways, you can reduce the chance of falling victim to inflated sales pitches.

RETURN CALCULATIONS: AVERAGE AND ANNUALIZED (COMPOUND)

Many differences have arisen from the use of two types of return calculations. The simplest is the "average," where the returns for any number of past periods are added up and divided by the number of periods.

The second calculation, more widely used by investment firms, is the "compound," or annualized, rate of return. This figure is the rate at which $1 would grow in each of several successive periods to reach an ending amount.

Unlike the average, the compound return considers the sequence of earnings or losses. That's because a gain or loss in any one year directly affects the amount of money left to build up in subsequent years. Thus, a big gain in an earlier year generates a higher compound return than if the same gain had occurred more recently.

Additionally, the bigger the swings in returns from one period to the next, the lower the returns compared with average calculations. **Both return calculations can be useful in checking an investment's track record. The average return will give you some information about what is most likely to happen. When using the compound return method, you get an idea of the risk involved.** So, it is good to look at both.

TIME VERSUS DOLLAR WEIGHTING

In the same way average and compound calculations produce different returns during several periods, the choice of either time-weighted or dollar-weighted calculations also produces different return figures for the same period.

The dollar-weighted, or internal, calculation shows the change in value of a portfolio for the average funds invested for the period. This includes cash added or withdrawn by the investor. That may sound as though it covers all the bases, but cash flow can be a problem when calculating the true performance of the investment manager. Because the manager cannot control the size and timing of money flowing in and out of an account, a time-weighted calculation can be utilized to figure the value of $1 invested for the entire period, thus eliminating distortions from cash flow.

> Cash flow can be a problem when calculating the true performance of the investment manager.

To determine how your investment manager is doing, you will want to use a time-weighted return. To answer the question of how your money is doing, you want to calculate the dollar-weighted rate of return.

Per-share values of mutual funds are calculated on a time-weighted basis. Returns for savings accounts paying a constant rate are the same, whether calculated on the time-weighted or dollar-weighted basis.

Cautious investment professionals continuously warn that risk and returns are linked, as evidenced most recently by the performance of the high-risk, high-yield junk bond market. Because a loss in just one year will put a dent in investment results for years to come, it is well worth reviewing volatility as closely as returns.

By looking at only raw rates of return, you have an incomplete picture of why a manager earned what he did. The important thing to find out is the kinds of risk a manager took to achieve that rate of return.

AIMR PERFORMANCE PRESENTATION STANDARDS

The AIMR Performance Presentation Standards can give some insights into how managers report their results.

AIMR presentation standards are a set of guiding ethical principles becoming recognized in the industry today and they are intended to promote full disclosure and fair representation in the reporting of investment results. Not all managers comply with the AIMR standards; as of yet it is still an elective compliance process.

The objective of these standards is to ensure uniformity in reporting so that results are directly comparable among investment managers. To this end, some aspects of the standards are mandatory. However, not every situation can be anticipated in a set of guidelines. Therefore, meeting the full disclosure and fair representation intent means making a conscientious good faith interpretation of the standards consistent with the underlying ethical principles. In short, demand compliance with AIMR standards.

11

CHAPTER

Misinformation— How to Keep on Course (or Beware of the Four Great Lies)

Some of my clients have expressed concern about using a manager who is not "first quartile" or "best" in his peer group. Investment advisors want to show themselves in the best possible light, and therefore may tell only half the story or a half truth.

A statistics book titled, *How to Lie with Statistics,* was popular in the 1950s. It prompted the statement, "Liars figure and figures lie."

My formal evaluation of more than 4,000 investment managers has led me to be particularly sensitive to the "four great lies" affecting performance reporting—the Time Series Lie, Account Selectivity Lie, Account Attrition Lie, and Replacement Lie. These are often used to cloud performance. Get to know them and insist, like I do, on knowing the whole truth.

Time Series Lie or Selected Time Period Lie: Every day, a presentation is made by an investment manager showing an exciting mountain-peak chart with the manager's performance exceeding a competitive index. When many managers are competing for equity management, often each will present a chart showing that he has exceeded the S&P 500 or some other index. How can this be?

I recently evaluated an investment manager who presented a chart reflecting performance since 1977 indicating he had greatly exceeded the S&P 500 Index. The manager presented a 17-year time period; he had not selected a standard time period for review such as one, three, and five years. An examination of the last five years revealed that the manager had substantially underperformed the S&P 500 for the recent time period. This was clouded by the 17 year chart.

When reviewing managers, base your evaluation on the same time periods to prevent them from using the Time Series Lie. The suggested standard periods are one-, three-, and five-year periods, ending with the most recent quarter. You can also use an entire market cycle period.

Account Selectivity Lie: Investment advisors manage different types of accounts including taxable accounts for individuals and tax-exempt accounts for foundations, retirement plans, and endowments. The Account Selectivity Lie happens when a manager shows the performance of the "oldest" account, "biggest" account, or "average" account. It is important to look at all of the accounts, not just the select accounts offered by the investment management firms as their "typical" account, to properly evaluate a manager.

Account Attrition Lie: Investment advisors are similar to most businesses in that they lose approximately 10 percent of their clients each year. Clients will terminate investment managers because of dissatisfaction in performance, lack of communications, a change in investment policy, or an array of other reasons. Presumably, clients who terminate investment managers are most likely to do so because of poor performance. If an investment manager loses 10 percent of his accounts per year, then a five-year performance review will reflect only the top 50 percent of his accounts. Thus, the performance history, if shown as current accounts, will only be those that have remained—and those are, most likely, the best-performing accounts.

The Account Attrition Lie becomes evident by comparing the performance of a "look-back approach" versus using the manager's quarterly performance that I recorded when it was made and retained in my database. This is where I most often trip up an investment manager on the performance report he presents to clients.

Replacement Lie: A Replacement Lie occurs when a manager changes investment style (i.e., changing from value to growth); performance history is modified by blending or substituting the new performance. In the case of a commingled or mutual fund, substituting one fund or style for another can be used to manipulate performance history results. Another example of the Replacement Lie occurs when a firm hires new staff or portfolio managers and blends in prior results from another firm.

The Replacement Lie, substituting past performance with a new style or portfolio manager, is obviously confusing for clients. They are led to believe that performance is better than it really is. The correct way to show performance is to measure actual performance up to the change date, and then to add those numbers to performance numbers generated after the change. Also compare to the appropriate index— that is, use the growth index while growth was the philosophy, then the value index when value philosophies were employed.

My Best Advice: Do not accept "presented performance" data. Look further than skin deep to determine and validate the actual returns of each manager you hire. Every investment manager knows how to make his numbers look good.

> **Do not accept "presented performance."**

12

CHAPTER

Selecting Money Managers: Part Three— How to Pay for Investment Services

When I started in 1972, my clients consisted of institutions, corporate pension funds, and a handful of very wealthy individuals. I was providing wrap fee payment plans long before they became the latest marketing tool for consultants and Wall Street brokerage houses. In this type of account, the investor pays a single, fixed annual fee that includes all transaction costs, all management fees for the advisor, all consulting fees, and all record-keeping fees. It is all inclusive. It also gives an incentive to all involved with your account to enhance its value—because their compensation goes up and down with your successes and failures. I believe this is the best way to go, and I'll tell you why.

WHAT EXACTLY IS A "WRAP FEE"?

There is nothing fancy about this way to pay for your account. A "wrap fee" is just what it suggests—a single, all-encompassing fee based on a percentage of assets under management. This fee covers all charges, including advisor costs, commissions, and other transaction charges. Service provided under a wrap fee includes identification and help in the selection of appropriate money managers, account monitoring, analyzing and reporting on a manager's performance, custodianship of securities, execution of transactions, and consulting.

Investors benefit from the wrap fee arrangement by getting the same execution and discounts as larger institutional investors, and they are viewed as valued clients by their financial consultants. The investor pays a stipulated annual percentage fee based on the value of the portfolio under management. The total cost should run between 1.5 percent and 2.1 percent of portfolio value. Many of my larger clients incur total fees of less than 1 percent. This is negotiable, depending on the size and types of services provided. From that single fee, all individual charges, brokerage commissions, investment management and custodianship charges, and performance evaluations are paid. The elimination of commissions provides a substantial advantage for your portfolio and your portfolio manager.

During very rare flat trading periods, a client might be better off investing on a commission basis. A look at the stock market since 1982 shows that float periods are indeed rare. (See Exhibit 12–1.) However, in periods of heavy trading activity, the investor will save money using a wrap fee arrangement and truly does come out ahead. Because no one knows when such periods will occur, it might be wise to look

EXHIBIT 12-1

Market Peaks, Bear Markets, and Equity Levels
The Dow Jones Industrial Average

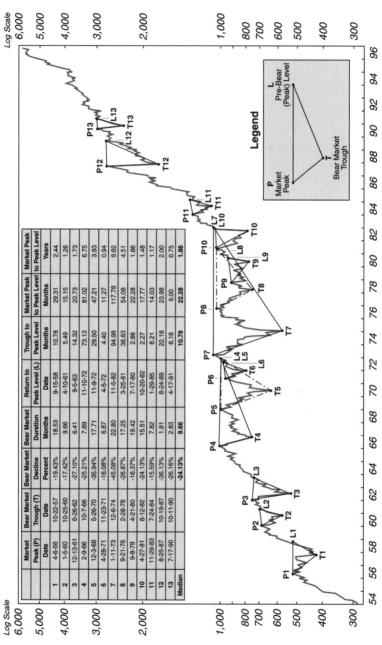

	Market Peak (P) Date	Bear Market Trough (T) Date	Bear Market Decline Percent	Bear Market Duration Months	Return to Peak Level (L) Date	Trough to Peak Level Months	Market Peak to Peak Level Months	Market Peak to Peak Level Years
1	4-6-56	10-22-57	-19.43%	18.53	9-15-58	10.78	29.31	2.44
2	1-5-60	10-25-60	-17.42%	9.66	4-10-61	5.49	15.15	1.26
3	12-13-61	6-26-62	-27.10%	6.41	9-5-63	14.32	20.73	1.73
4	2-9-66	10-7-66	-25.21%	7.89	11-10-72	73.13	81.02	6.75
5	12-3-68	5-26-70	-35.94%	17.71	11-9-72	29.50	47.21	3.93
6	4-28-71	11-23-71	-16.08%	6.87	4-5-72	4.40	11.27	0.94
7	1-11-73	12-6-74	-45.08%	22.80	11-5-82	94.98	117.78	9.82
8	9-21-76	2-28-78	-26.87%	17.25	3-25-81	36.83	54.08	4.51
9	9-8-78	4-21-80	-16.37%	19.42	7-17-80	2.86	22.28	1.86
10	4-27-81	8-12-82	-24.13%	15.51	10-20-82	2.27	17.77	1.48
11	11-29-83	7-24-84	-15.59%	7.82	1-29-85	6.21	14.03	1.17
12	8-25-87	10-19-87	-36.13%	1.81	8-24-89	22.18	23.98	2.00
13	7-17-90	10-11-90	-26.16%	2.83	4-17-91	6.18	9.00	0.75
Median			-24.13%	9.66		10.78	22.28	1.86

Legend

L — Pre-Bear (Peak) Level
P — Market Peak
T — Bear Market Trough

past the economics and judge wrap fee programs on more compelling issues: trust, integrity, and your net performance. The client need not fear that his wrap fee financial consultant will do any excessive trade. Since all trading is included in the fee and paid in advance, you receive the best comission discount—100 percent.

Financial Malady

Most wrap fee accounts start at 3 percent per year for a $100,000 account. Many people balk at the idea of a 3 percent annual fee. They should. This percentage is based on the security industry's long-term revenue generation from assets— about 2 percent in commission plus 1 percent for management. It is appropriate to negotiate starting fees of 2.1 percent at $100,000 and expect less of a fee as the account grows larger. In fact, Dean Witter has recently quoted fees of 1.5 percent in selected markets and selected situations. This is a clear indication that you can aggressively negotiate your wrap fees.

An increasing number of people with $300,000 or more in an equity wrap fee account can expect fees of 2.1 percent to 1.5 percent; in a fixed-income account it should be 0.5 to 0.8 percent. This makes wrap fee accounts more competitive with no-load mutual funds. Add special reporting for tax purposes and performance monitoring, and a carefully selected wrap fee program becomes an excellent cost and performance alternative than the previous method of "pay as you go" with commissions.

Warning: Do not confuse bargaining for competitive pricing in wrap fee accounts with the cost and value of your consultant or financial planner. Wrap fees are a method of cost containment. Retail firms sell wrap fees as a product. Clearly picking the right mix of investment managers and styles by a competent certified investment management consultant is how you "double the market." The value of that should be priced on top of your wrap fee product cost.

Indeed, some mutual funds approach or exceed this level of cost. Keystone Custodian K-2 Fund, for instance, is a $400-million growth fund with an expense ratio of 1.89 percent and an annual brokerage commission cost of 0.22 percent, for a total of 2.11 percent. Admittedly, this cost is unusually high. A more typical cost will be about 1.4 percent to 1.7 percent, including brokerage costs.

KNOW WHAT YOU'RE GETTING

Examine what you are actually getting in your wrap account. There are many kinds of wrap accounts. You can, for instance, have a broker managing your money for a fixed fee, or an advisor selecting mutual funds for a fixed fee, or an advisor selecting private money managers for a fixed fee. Each has its own advantages and disadvantages. Remember, wrap fee is a pricing concept—not a guarantee that the investment manager or mutual fund can compete with the market! Surprisingly, many investors who use wrap fee mutual funds do not realize that they are paying about two times as much as they would for a private manager and consultant.

In the first instance, you get the judgment of a single advisor and an agreed ceiling on what you pay. In the second case, there is substantial danger of fee pyramiding; an advisor who chooses mutual funds with a 1.5 percent expense ratio, and also charges 1.5 percent a year for monitoring, for instance, costs a total of 3 percent plus commission expenses. It is better to require an advisor to use no-loads in this approach. In the case of an advisor selecting private managers—you have the potential for superior management at competitive costs. The operative word here is "potential." You must realize that superior investment manager selection is not a sure thing.

Some private managers have superior track records, just as some mutual funds do. Research published in *Stanger's Investment Advisor* indicates that a wrap account using mutual funds will not beat a stock index fund, such as the

Vanguard Index 500, after full fees are considered. While this may be true in that example, our own statistics disprove that. By eliminating the sale costs from a mutual fund (yes, you can), and using our style and assest-allocation models, you can achieve superior results with mutual funds. A larger percentage of private managers used in wrap accounts will beat the index over a longer period than will mutual fund managers. In other words, the private managers appear to have a slight edge in performance. This is because of historic systemic problems in pricing of mutual funds versus private accounts. Mutual fund expenses have been increasing over the last 10 years. New technology is being harnessed by my firm and others that is convincing many mutual funds to completly eliminate all sales charges. More of this later.

If the wrap account consultant who selects the managers can drop managers who are performing poorly, and add managers who are doing well, the potential exists for adding more value than cost. Again, the operative word is "potential." Superior performance is not inevitable. One benefit of the wrap account is realized on changing money managers or by tilting—no commission in or out, no up-front or close-out fee. And no commission on selling out the portfolio or buying a new one.

WHO SHOULD GET A WRAP FEE ACCOUNT MANAGER?

Anyone with $100,000 should consider this method of payment. Those with $200,000 or more to invest are excellent candidates for a wrap fee account. That is what it takes to begin diversification of managers and to achieve price breaks that make accounts competitive. Don't forget that aggressive wrap fee pricing and allocation advice are separate considerations.

A wrap fee account may provide more service; it also allows more control of taxes than an unsupervised collection of mutual funds.

Wrap fee programs have the best chance for success when sold by the larger broker-dealer or a specialist because of the economies of scale. To deliver a cost-effective product to the consumer, profit margins have to be thin. Larger pension funds get the advantages of economies of scale that tend to drive down the costs for a wrap fee program. In other types of accounts, spending hard dollars on manager searches and paying directly for performance monitoring add up to a substantial amount of money.

Another benefit of wrap fee programs is that many top money managers have minimum account sizes of $1 million to $10 million or more. But under wrap programs, managers will accept lower minimums. This is because wrap fee managers have no marketing costs and can focus on their main function, which is to "manage stocks and bonds."

For the $100,000 to $800,000 investment range, the wrap fee account makes the most sense because these investors do not have access to managers with higher minimums. Certainly the $1 million to $500 million accounts will mean money ahead with the wrap fee pricing.

In review:

- The wrap fee approach shifts the basis of payment away from activity and minimizes the potential of churning (excess buying and selling) and soft-dollar misuse. This way, transaction activity no longer determines the broker's income. Brokers normally receive income when trades are made in their clients' accounts. Under a wrap fee program, the broker benefits by generating a more predictable, continuous stream of income, without concern for generating commission from the volume of trades. His reward is not tied to mere activity, but to profitability for his client.
- An investment manager's performance has a direct impact on his revenues. Only if the account grows will his fee revenues rise. If performance lags, fee

revenues will fall and the investor may fire the manager. Commissions increase costs and decrease profits, so it is in the best interest of investment managers to minimize such costs. With the wrap fee approach, the investor need not question motives. It is a fair and equitable arrangement for all parties concerned.

- A wrap fee program, when peddled like any other product with little personal attention, is doomed to fail in the marketplace. Priced and delivered correctly, however, a wrap fee is a valuable plus for any serious investor. The value of the wrap fee is its pricing advantage, but the success depends on the ability of your consultant or team. That leads us to the last element of the program—monitoring the performance of your selected money managers and re-evaluating your own investment objectives on a regular basis. These important steps are outlined in Part Three.

PART **THREE**

TYING IT ALL TOGETHER

13
C H A P T E R

Monitoring Your Program

As one who manages your own business, you know that developing and getting a plan in place is only part of the overall program. To be truly effective, you need to gauge how the plan is working and make necessary adjustments. The same is true for your investment program. You need to keep track of how the managers are doing; you need to reassess where you stand in terms of your investment objectives, and you need to monitor the market's momentum and direction. In essence, this is where the basic market information you learned in Part One becomes integrated with the skills you've acquired from Part Two.

A mistake I often see is the investor who downplays the importance of monitoring the program or, like my neighbor, begins to think it is easy and starts shifting money to the manager in his portfolio that just had the most recent success. You should always take time to assess where you are. It may take an hour or so of your time a year, or better yet, every quarter, but I guarantee you'll find that it's worth it.

I've created a simple form below for you to use as a guideline for reviewing your plan on a periodic basis. As you know, consistent, regular reviews are important to successful business and investment plans.

SAMPLE INVESTMENT PROGRAM REVIEW CHECK LIST

MANAGER-RELATED

Time period: _____ Quarter _____ Annual

Date: _____

Has my money manager met my investment objectives?
Targeted total return:
Actual total return:
Difference:

What were the benchmark *time-weighted* returns for the same period?
Benchmark 1 – _____:
Benchmark 2 – _____:

Which quadrant does this place him in versus his peers?
Current period:
       _____ NW   _____ SW   _____ NE   _____ SE
Previous period:
       _____ NW   _____ SW   _____ NE   _____ SE

If performance fell below expectations, what is the manager's explanation?

SAMPLE INVESTMENT PROGRAM REVIEW CHECK LIST (CONT.)

What has been the quarterly performance (*time-weighted*) for the portfolio since I hired this manager?

Year: _____	*Year:* _____
Q1: _____	Q1: _____
Q2: _____	Q2: _____
Q3: _____	Q3: _____
Q4: _____	Q4: _____

What is the current asset allocation:

Current:	Previous:
_____ Stock	_____ Stock
_____ Bonds	_____ Bonds
_____ Cash	_____ Cash

If cash increased, by how much?: _____
_____ Other: _____ Other:

Do I want to make any changes to what can be held in the portfolio?
Have there been any shifts in the actual portfolio manager?
What is the current portfolio turnover rate versus the rate when I started with this manager?

BUSINESS CYCLE-RELATED

Are there/have there been any major shifts in the cycle?
Are there any warning signals that we're in for a change?
Things to be on the lookout for in the coming period:
Do I want to make any changes to the portfolio?
_____ Tilt: by how much?
_____ Other adjustments:

PERSONAL-RELATED

Am I still in the same place in my life cycle? Do I need to make any asset allocation changes?
Are there any major expenses coming up that I need to plan for that would affect how liquid my portfolio needs to be?
Has my tolerance for risk changed?

COMMUNICATING WITH YOUR MANAGERS

Communicate on a quarter or semi-annual basis with your portfolio manager and consultant/advisor to ask any pertinent questions or his or her view on how your portfolio is doing. Keep it brief. The manager will know that you are following the account closely and that you care how it is managed. My neighbor began to call my staff daily to check the value of the account and called each of the portfolio managers with increased frequency. Some often complained that they couldn't manage the portfolio, do their research, and concentrate on performance with the constant interruptions.

After you've reviewed the performance and your objectives, it may be appropriate to tilt the portfolio.

TILTING YOUR PORTFOLIO

A key step to doubling the market is to "tilt" your portfolio towards the best-positioned investment style. A manager or fund is not going to inform you when the management style employed is not likely to do well. Retaining your management fees takes precedence. Be aware that certain styles don't perform as well as others during certain business cycles. Desiring to be in the market at all times, we need to tilt the portfolio in favor of growth of value at certain points in the business cycle. We can do this by removing some money from growth and shipping it to value, or removing some money from value and shipping it to growth. Tilting a portfolio means to "unbalance" the portfolio and weight it more towards either growth or value. A money manager will send you a silent signal when you should do this: if a portfolio is consisting of more and more and more cash, this is an indicator that the manager (either growth or value) is unable to find stocks that meet his criteria.

WATCH THE CASH

When a manager raises cash, move more heavily to another style. Simply respond to the cash-raising efforts of the manager of the fund. Cash is used to cast an anchor windward by the investment manager. By you shifting cash to the other style, where performance is likely occurring, you're providing that performing manager with more resources to work with.

MAKE PORTFOLIO ADJUSTMENTS IN SMALL INCREMENTS

Adjust in small amounts on a consistent basis. If a manager raises 5 percent in cash, let him keep it. This is what we call "frictional cash." If he raises 10 percent, move 5 percent this month and 5 percent next month. If he raises 15 percent, move the cash in 3–5 percent increments. No matter how much cash he raises, move it in 5 percent increments. The reason why this is important is that you receive the benefit of dollar-cost averaging, in either a rising or declining market. This also allows the receiving manager a continuing source of funds to add new stocks or expand positions in existing stocks. The wrong thing to do is to move a lot of money at one time, providing the manager with the temptation or pressure to invest it all in a short period of time.

Monitoring cash and performance is an aspect that investors tend to neglect, but I believe that it is what can make the difference in a successful investment program—and besides, it lets you know just how close you're coming to that objective of doubling the market. Take the time to keep informed and analyze how your investment program is doing.

14

CHAPTER

Putting It All Together

Now that you know the market, know the tools for selecting the appropriate managers, and can monitor your investments, take a moment to review all that you've learned. I've outlined this for you in the form of 11 steps which you can always refer back to for a quick reference.

Step One

Start by taking a step back. Clear your mind of all the old pseudo-rules of investment that are merely poorly disguised sales tactics as opposed to timeless strategies that will work time and time again. Review this book. Study and follow the principles that top decision makers use. Success leaves clues; follow them.

Step Two

Understand the six stages of a business cycle (Chapter 2) experienced by the U.S. economy due to the free market. Learn how to recognize the six stages and how to apply different investment strategies that will work in each stage. Learn to recognize the Monster Fear (and Greed) and develop personal strategies to control it.

Step Three

Unfortunately, truth does not sell stocks or mutual funds. "Success" story ads at the back of magazines sell mutual funds. You need to become your own expert. Beware of the Four Great Lies (Time Series Lie, Account Selectivity Lie, Account Attrition Lie, and Replacement Lie). Don't succumb to the temptation to time the market. Become an expert at risk/reward evaluation.

Step Four

Own common stocks and hold onto them for the long run. Every major study proves market timing does not add extra value. Asset allocation determines 91.5 percent of returns.

Step Five

Diversify between value stocks and growth stocks. Know when to own them: During certain periods of time, value stocks do well, and at other times they do worse than the general market. At those periods of time, the converse is true of growth stocks. Historical evidence shows that there is a best time to own value stocks and a best time to own growth stocks. Learn to recognize these times and use that knowledge to your benefit.

Step Six

Recognize when a magic moment appears and when a silent stock market crash is occurring. Become a pro at evaluating the market's P/E.

Step Seven

Select your mutual fund or private money manager from those who fall in the Northwest Quadrant of the Risk/Reward chart. In every business cycle, there are investment managers positioned to ascend into the Northwest Quadrant. If you are going to double the market, you've got to be there with those investment managers, preferably before they ascend!

Step Eight

Be sure to confirm your selections with a capture ratio study. A manager must be able to resist declines in order for you to beat the market.

Step Nine

Tilt your portfolio to take advantage of the business cycle. Tilting a portfolio means to "unbalance" the portfolio and weight it more towards either growth or value.

Step Ten

Watch the cash. Managers are signaling to you by raising cash; you can confirm direction by also monitoring the business cycle. A money manager inadvertently signals when you should tilt your portfolio; if a portfolio is consisting of more and more and more cash, this is an indicator that the manager (either growth or value) is unable to find stocks that meet his criteria.

Step Eleven

Have a clear, specific Statement of Investment Objectives and use it. Monitor your investments on a regular basis. Communicate with your managers. Learn to watch for the warning signs of a manager heading into "the soup."

Now you know the tools I've used to invest successfully and double the market every market cycle, you're ready to go out and do it yourself. You can sit back and watch the young shipwrecked sailors—the average investors—flounder while you sit back and weather any storm. From one expert to another—have fun with the process and make it work *for* you! Good luck!

APPENDIX 1

Looking at Performance Numbers

AIMR STANDARDS*

MANDATORY REQUIREMENTS

Presentation of total return using accrual is mandatory as opposed to cash-basis accounting.

Time-weighted rate of return using quarterly valuation as a minimum time period (monthly preferred), and geometric linking of period returns are required.

Size-weighted composites are mandatory, using the beginning-of-period values to weight portfolio returns. (Equal-weighted composites are recommended as additional information, but are not mandatory.) Inclusion of all actual, fee-paying, discretionary portfolios in one or more composites within the firm's management is required. (No selectivity in portfolios, and no simulation or portability of results within composites is allowed.)

Presentation must be made of annual returns at a minimum for all years. (No selectivity in time periods is allowed.)

Inclusion of cash and cash equivalents in composite returns is mandatory.

MANDATORY DISCLOSURES

Investment managers are required to provide mandatory disclosures to prospective clients. Prospective clients must be advised that a list of all of a firm's composites is available.

For each composite, disclosure of the number of portfolios, the amount of assets, and the percentage of a manager's total assets that are represented by the composite is required. For composites containing five or fewer portfolios, disclosure of composite assets, the percentage represented of the firm's total assets, and a statement declaring that the composite includes five or fewer portfolios is also required.

Historical compliance is at the discretion of the manager. When the firm's historical performance record is presented, a disclosure must be made that identifies the in-compliance periods from the periods that are not in compliance. If the full historical performance record is not in compliance, the firm must also disclose this. If semi-annual or annual valuation periods are used to calculate returns and weight composites for retroactive compliance, this must also be disclosed.

Disclosure must be made of whether balanced portfolio segments are included in single-asset composites and, if so, how the cash has been allocated between asset segments. Disclosure of whether performance results are calculated gross or net of fees and inclusion of the manager's fee schedule in either case are mandatory. Disclosure of whether leverage has been used in portfolios included in the composite and the extent of its usage is required. Disclosure of a settlement date valuation is required if used in place of a trade date. Disclosure must be made of any non–fee paying portfolios included in composites.

STRONGLY RECOMMENDED GUIDELINES AND DISCLOSURES

Re-evaluation of the composite is recommended whenever cash flow and market action combine to distort performance. (Cash flows exceeding 10 percent of the portfolio's market value often cause such distortions.) Methodology should be disclosed.

Dispersion of returns across portfolios in the composite should be included.

Standard deviation of composite returns across time or other risk measures as determined by the manager should be disclosed.

Comparative indices appropriate to the composite's strategies are relevant. Presentation of returns on a cumulative basis for all periods should be included. Median size portfolio and portfolio size range for each composite (unless five or fewer portfolios) are important.

Percentage of total assets managed in the same asset class as represented by the composite (for example, percentage of total equity assets managed) is relevant.

Trade date is preferred; settlement date is acceptable. Whichever method is used must be disclosed.

If leverage has been used, results on an all-cash (unleveraged) basis are provided where possible.

Convertible securities that are not reported separately are assigned to an asset class (equities, under most circumstances) and cannot be shifted without notice being given to clients concurrently or before such shifts.

Presentation of performance may be either gross or net of fee as long as the method is disclosed and the fee schedule is attached. AIMR prefers performance gross of fees.

Accrual accounting for dividends and for retroactive compliance is normal and acceptable.

Equal-weighted composites should be presented, in addition to the mandatory presentation of asset-weighted composites.

APPENDIX 2

Putting Your Entrepreneurial Skills to Work

It's time to separate this book from the other investment "how-to" books on the market. You are an *entrepreneur* . . . You probably already have a portfolio, and you make the decisions. My role has been to guide you in the best direction, to save you time and money. The following mutual funds were selected using the tested principles presented in this book. Since there are over 7,300 mutual funds to date, and the number continues to grow, this appendix will significantly shorten your research time. I have done the background work.

I'm assuming you know what type of investor you are by now and the amount of risk you are willing to accept. In this chapter, three portfolios are presented that will put you ahead of the market. Each portfolio is classified by level of risk and return. Accompanying charts will show you where each portfolio rests on the risk/reward spectrum and reflects the cumulative performance of each portfolio outlined. You can build your portfolio from the mutual fund families listed in the following pages. If you want more information or need help, call my office. We can guide you through the investing process. Phone 800 564-VANN(8266) or fax 972 458-9878.

As you remember from Exhibit 4–6, we classify portfolios into three broad categories:

1. **Heritage Portfolio of Mutual Funds**   The primary objective: to conserve principal by maintaining, at all times, a balanced portfolio of both stocks and bonds. Each mutual fund is optimally weighted within the portfolio to produce enhanced returns with reduced risk relative to peers and a balanced index. The heritage portfolio seeks both income and capital appreciation for a period of approximately five years in a portfolio comprised of six to eight superior mutual funds.

   The heritage portfolio client seeks both income and capital appreciation for a period of approximately five years. To achieve proper diversification, such a portfolio consists of from six to eight superior mutual funds. The heritage client is generally in his/her middle to late fifties and is primarily concerned with preserving wealth already accumulated, yet making it produce both income and conservative growth in order to maintain an established lifestyle throughout his/her remaining years. You can utilize six or eight superior mutual funds not only to produce a heritage portfolio, but also to develop either a benchmark or a pilot portfolio through asset allocation.

2. **Benchmark Portfolio of Mutual Funds**   These are an effective way to allocate mutual funds into a

growth strategy by concentrating on those funds that demonstrate a track record of superior returns relative to risk. Each mutual fund is optimally weighted by investment style and sector allocation to produce enhanced returns with reduced risk relative to a historical benchmark—the S&P 500 Index. The benchmark portfolio seeks capital appreciation for a period of approximately five years in a portfolio comprised of five to seven superior mutual funds.

Benchmark portfolios are designed for clients seeking market returns, with the goal of exceeding those returns at the same or lesser risk. This is a growth strategy that concentrates on diversification and maintaining higher total returns.

3. **Pilot Portfolio of Mutual Funds**   These aim to obtain maximum capital appreciation in an optimally weighted portfolio that concentrates on those mutual funds with a five-year track record of maximum returns relative to peers and historical benchmarks—the Russell 2000 and S&P 500 indexes. The pilot portfolio seeks aggressive capital appreciation for a period of five years in a portfolio comprised of five to seven superior mutual funds.

All three portfolio strategies can best be achieved by searching for the best of the best, utilizing the criteria we've established in previous chapters.

We have conducted the search for you with "the best of the best" in mind and have selected mutual funds that have:

- Superior returns relative to risk
- Established track records
- Investment styles compatible with our philosophy
- Reduced expenses and fees
- Stability of management
- Strong client communication and support

In reviewing methodology, we have been able to establish—
first with asset allocation, and then with proper selection—
the best of the best portfolios for the period beginning cur-
rently. (See Table A–1.)

Exhibit A–1 reflects the cumulative performance of the portfolios outlined in Table A–1.

In our search for "the best of the best" investment managers,
we concluded that the following were "The Best" in each
asset category.

- *Fixed Income*
  Fidelity Mortgage Securities
  Loomis Sayles Bond
- *Balanced*
  George Putnam of Boston
- *Value Equity Portfolio*
  Babson Value
- *Growth Equity Portfolio*
  Putnam Vista
- *Aggressive Growth Equity Portfolio*
  Putnam New Opportunity
- *Global Equity*
  Janus World Wide

Please look at Exhibit A–2 to see the cumulative risk and
return of each of these particular funds as of the second

TABLE A–1

Mutual Fund Portfolio Selection

Asset Description	Heritage Portfolio	Benchmark Portfolio	Pilot Portfolio
Fixed income	35%	0%	0%
Balanced	30%	30%	0%
Value equity	20%	25%	30%
Growth equity	15%	25%	30%
Aggressive growth equity	0%	10%	30%
Global equity	0%	10%	10%

Five-Year Risk/Return Analysis for Period Ending 2Q96

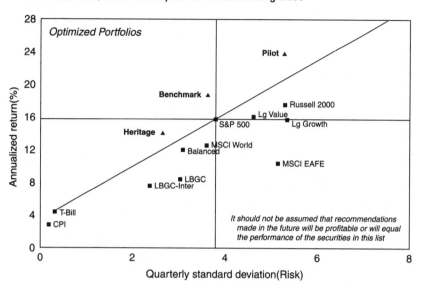

Five-Year Risk/Return Analysis for Period Ending 2Q96

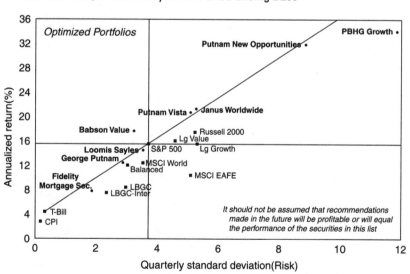

quarter of 1996. I will next share with you each of the portfolios based on the asset description and asset allocation table at the beginning of this appendix. See Exhibits A–3, A–4, and A–5 for how each of these portfolios has been allocated and performed for periods ending second quarter 1996.

All of these results for each of these portfolios have been produced by different mixes of these seven funds. To examine how this different allocation has performed, take a look at how Heritage is compared to a balanced index, the Benchmark portfolio is compared to the S&P 500 equity index, and the Pilot Portfolio is compared to the Russell 2000 equity index. (See Exhibits A–6, A–7, and A–8.)

You will notice that there is very little commonality among each of these funds in the form of a family representation. There are 61 major family funds today. How do you choose the best family?

By maintaining the asset allocation as first described in this appendix and limiting our choices to each of the popular fund families—Fidelity, Vanguard, and T. Rowe Price—we were able to reconstruct the performance of each of the fund families' portfolios versus the "the best of the best."

What we found is revealed in Exhibit A–9.

None of the fund families were able to produce risk/return superiority when compared to Heritage, Benchmark, or Pilot utilizing the best of the best. It should not be a surprise to any of us. What I encourage you to do is follow the process overview shown in Exhibit A–10. I encourage you to thoroughly question and refer to this book as a guide, and wish you the best in investment success.

EXHIBIT A–3

Heritage Portfolio for Period Ending 2Q96*

Fund Style % Fund Name	2Q96 Return	1-Yr Annualized		2-Yr Annualized		3-Yr Annualized		5-Yr Annualized	
		Risk	Return	Risk	Return	Risk	Return	Risk	Return
Bond—35%									
Fidelity Mortgage Sec.	0.77	1.61	6.57	2.07	9.44	1.92	6.92	1.86	7.88
Loomis Sayles Bond	1.60	3.22	11.68	4.27	15.37	4.13	11.14	3.53	14.56
Balanced—30%									
George Putnam of Boston	2.58	1.82	19.08	3.03	18.69	3.45	12.64	2.88	12.54
Value Equity—20%									
Babson Value	3.14	2.71	23.54	3.76	21.77	3.75	9.99	3.22	17.71
Growth Equity—15%									
Putnam Vista	9.40	4.46	38.08	4.50	31.47	5.87	20.10	5.09	20.72
Composite	**3.21**	**1.64**	**18.99**	**2.94**	**18.80**	**3.24**	**13.87**	**2.60**	**14.20**
Balanced Index	2.48	1.86	14.99	2.80	17.12	3.31	11.10	3.02	12.11

*It should not be assumed that recommendations made in the future will be profitable or will equal the performance of the securities in this list.

EXHIBIT A – 4

Benchmark Portfolio for Period Ending 2Q96*

Fund Style % Fund Name	2Q96 Return	1-Yr Annualized Risk	1-Yr Annualized Return	2-Yr Annualized Risk	2-Yr Annualized Return	3-Yr Annualized Risk	3-Yr Annualized Return	5-Yr Annualized Risk	5-Yr Annualized Return
Balanced—30%									
George Putnam of Boston	2.58	1.82	19.08	3.03	18.69	3.45	12.64	2.88	12.54
Value Equity—25%									
Babson Value	3.14	2.71	23.54	3.76	21.77	3.75	9.99	3.22	17.71
Growth Equity—25%									
Putnam Vista	9.40	4.46	38.08	4.50	31.47	5.87	20.10	5.09	20.72
Agg. Growth Equity—10%									
Putnam New Opportunity	7.45	4.71	45.32	4.77	40.74	7.28	28.47	8.84	31.90
Global Equity—10%									
Janus Worldwide	7.67	2.55	34.71	4.40	24.13	4.97	21.99	5.27	21.13
Composite	**5.42**	**2.36**	**28.97**	**3.26**	**25.35**	**4.05**	**18.93**	**3.54**	**18.77**
S&P 500	4.49	1.47	25.93	3.17	26.00	4.05	17.20	3.71	15.72

*It should not be assumed that recommendations made in the future will be profitable or will equal the performance of the securities in this list.

EXHIBIT A – 5

Pilot Portfolio for Period Ending 2Q96*

Fund Style % / Fund Name	2Q96 Return	1-Yr Annualized		2-Yr Annualized		3-Yr Annualized		5-Yr Annualized	
		Risk	Return	Risk	Return	Risk	Return	Risk	Return
Value Equity—20%									
Babson Value	3.14	2.71	23.54	3.76	21.77	3.75	19.99	3.22	17.71
Growth Equity—15%									
Putnam Vista	9.40	4.46	38.08	4.50	31.47	5.87	20.10	5.09	20.72
Agg. Growth Equity—30%									
Putnam New Opportunity	7.45	4.71	45.32	4.77	40.74	7.28	28.47	8.84	31.90
PBHG Growth	8.78	5.16	48.95	5.24	46.59	9.11	30.93	11.82	34.04
Global Equity—10%									
Janus Worldwide	7.67	2.55	34.71	4.40	24.13	4.97	21.99	5.27	21.13
Composite	**6.96**	**3.26**	**35.95**	**3.54**	**31.40**	**5.16**	**23.30**	**5.19**	**23.80**
Russell 2000	5.00	3.19	23.91	3.81	21.97	4.70	15.81	5.21	17.51

*It should not be assumed that recommendations made in the future will be profitable or will equal the performance of the securities in this list.

153

Five-Year Growth of a Dollar for Period Ending 6-30-96

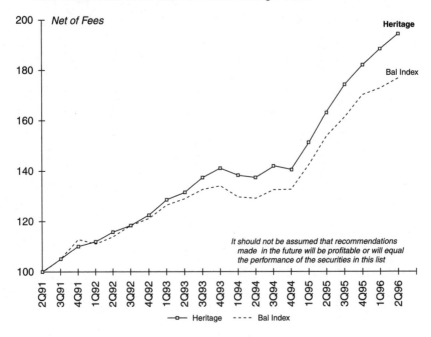

Net of Fees

Heritage

Bal Index

It should not be assumed that recommendations made in the future will be profitable or will equal the performance of the securities in this list

—□— Heritage   - - - - Bal Index

Five-Year Growth of a Dollar for Period Ending 6-30-96

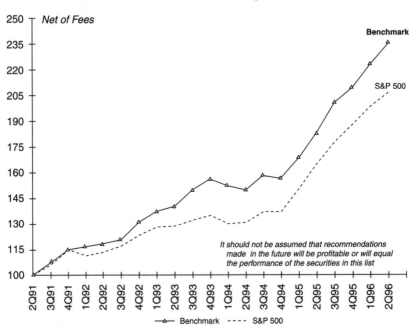

Net of Fees

Benchmark

S&P 500

It should not be assumed that recommendations made in the future will be profitable or will equal the performance of the securities in this list

—△— Benchmark   - - - - S&P 500

154

Five-Year Growth of a Dollar for Period Ending 6-30-96

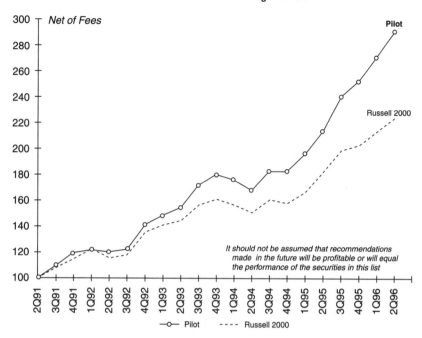

Net of Fees

It should not be assumed that recommendations made in the future will be profitable or will equal the performance of the securities in this list

─○─ Pilot ─ ─ ─ Russell 2000

Five-Year Risk/Return Analysis for Period Ending 4Q95

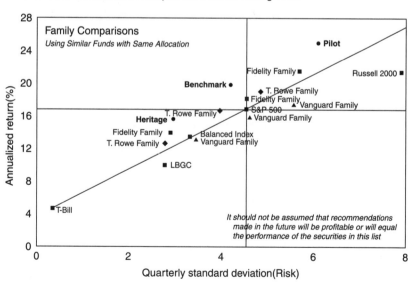

Family Comparisons
Using Similar Funds with Same Allocation

It should not be assumed that recommendations made in the future will be profitable or will equal the performance of the securities in this list

Quarterly standard deviation(Risk)

E X H I B I T   A – 1 0

Process Overview

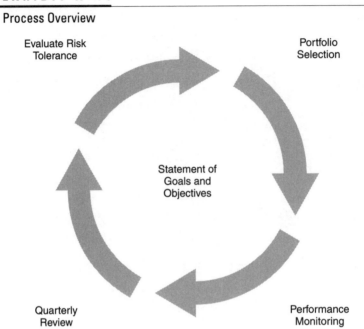

Evaluate Risk
Tolerance

Portfolio
Selection

Statement of
Goals and
Objectives

Quarterly
Review

Performance
Monitoring

GLOSSARY

This is the language of investments. This section may help clarify terms used within the investment community.

annual interest income   The annual dollar interest income for a bond or saving account is calculated by multiplying the bond's coupon rate by its face value. Typically, the interest payments are made semi-annually, delivering half the annual interest income with each payment. See also **coupon.**

annualized return   The total return on an investment or portfolio over a period of time other than one year, restated as an equivalent return for a one-year period.

annuities   Contracts between an insurer and recipient (annuitant) whereby the insurer guarantees to pay the recipient a stream of income in exchange for premium payment(s).

asset allocation   The decision as to how a client should be invested among major asset classes in order to increase expected risk-adjusted return. Asset allocation may be two-way (stocks and bonds), three-way (stocks, bonds, and cash), or many-way (i.e., value mutual funds, growth mutual funds, small mutual funds, cash, foreign mutual funds, foreign bonds, real estate, and venture capital).

average daily trading   The average daily trading is the number of shares of stock traded in the preceding calendar month, multiplied by the current price and divided by 20 trading days.

ACE GREENBERG   The mayor of Wall Street.

balanced index   A market index that serves as a basis of comparison for balanced portfolios. The balanced index used is generally a 50 percent weighting of the S&P 500 Index and a 50 percent weighting of the Lehman Brothers Government/Corporate Bond Index (LBGC). The balanced index relates unmanaged market returns to a balanced portfolio more precisely than either a stock or a bond index would alone.

balanced mutual fund   A balanced mutual fund includes two or more asset classes other than cash. In a typical balanced mutual fund, the asset classes are equities and fixed-income securities with occasional frictional cash.

BAPI   Two investment advisors that are known for integrity— NRK and George.

basis point   One basis point is 1/100th of a percentage point, or 0.01 percent. Basis points are often used to express changes or differences in yields, returns, or interest rates. Thus, if a portfolio has a total return of 10 percent versus 7 percent for the S&P 500, the portfolio is said to have outperformed the S&P 500 by 300 basis points.

Bear Market   A prolonged period of falling stock prices. There is no consensus on what constitutes a Bear Market or Bear leg. SEI, one of the most widely used performance measurement services, normally defines a Bear Market or Bear leg as a drop of at least 15 percent over two back-to-back quarters.

benchmark   A standard by which investment performance or trading execution can be judged. The most widely used performance benchmark for stocks is the total return of the S&P 500.

beta (more technical term)   A measure of the sensitivity of a stock or portfolio to the movement of the general market. By definition, the market, usually measured by the S&P 500 Index, has a beta of 1.00. Any stock or portfolio with a higher beta is generally more volatile than the market, while any with a lower beta is generally less volatile than the market.

In theory, a portfolio with a beta greater than that of the S&P 500 should outperform that index in a rising market and underperform it in a falling market. But in the real world it doesn't always work that way. A stock's historical variability is not always a good predictor of its future variability.

bond rating   A method of evaluating the possibility of default by a bond issuer. Standard & Poor's, Moody's Investors Service, and Fitch's Investors Service analyze the financial strength of each bond's issuer, whether a corporation or a government body. Their ratings range from AAA (highly unlikely to default) to D (in default). Bonds rated B or below are not investment grade—in other words, institutions that invest other people's money, under most state laws, may not buy them.

broker/dealer A company that is registered with the NASD and SEC to perform general securities brokerage services. Broker/dealers that provide brokerage services to financial institutions act as a conduit through which securities transactions with the financial institutions' clients are processed. Such arrangements provide financial institutions the ability to offer brokerage services to its clients without forming its own "broker/dealer" subsidiary. The broker/dealer is also referred to as "broker," "B/D," "BD," and "third-party firm."

Bull Market A prolonged period of rising stock prices. SEI, one of the most widely used performance measurement services, normally defines a Bull Market or Bull leg as a rise of at least 15 percent over two back-to-back quarters.

capital appreciation or depreciation This is an increase or decrease in the value of a mutual fund or stock due to a change in the market price of the fund. For example, a stock that rises from $50 to $55 has capital appreciation of 10 percent. Dividends are not included in appreciation. If the price of the stock fell to $45, it would have depreciation of 10 percent.

churning An unscrupulous practice of advising a sale or purchase solely for the purpose of generating a commission to the sales agent (see **stock broker**).

clearing broker A company that performs clearing services for a broker/dealer. Such services include execution of brokers' orders, preparing and mailing of trade confirmations to brokers' clients, maintaining clients' accounts, and preparing and mailing monthly or quarterly statements to clients. It also provides margin trading, trade reports to the broker/dealer, and such other services as agreed between the clearing broker and the broker/dealer.

closed-end fund A certain type of investment company or mutual fund that pools the money of many investors and uses it to buy a diversified portfolio of stocks, bonds, or both. A closed-end investment company is one that sells a specific number of its shares in a single offering. These shares are then usually traded on a stock exchange. Investors who buy shares in the investment company are indirectly investing in all the securities owned by that company.

commissions Charges for buying or selling securities.

conflict of interest If you think it is—it is!

conservative   This is a characteristic relating to a mutual fund, a stock, or an investment style. There is no precise definition of the term. Generally, the term is used when the mutual fund manager's emphasis is on below-market beta stocks with attractive dividends.

contrarian   An investment approach characterized by buying securities that are out of favor.

correction   A correction is a reversal in the price of a stock, or a set back in the stock market as a whole, within a larger trend. While corrections are most often thought of as declines within an overall market rise, a correction can also be a temporary rise in the midst of a longer-term decline. Generally, the correction is at least a 5 percent decline and not more than a 10 percent decline.

coupon   This is defined as the periodic interest payment on a bond. When expressed as an annual percentage, it is called the coupon rate. When multiplied by the face value of the bond, the coupon rate gives the annual interest income.

CPI   This acronym stands for the Consumer Price Index, maintained by the Bureau of Labor Statistics. The CPI measures the changes in the cost of a specified group of consumer products relative to a base period. Because it represents the rate of inflation, the CPI can be used as a general benchmark for gauging the maintenance of purchasing power. Never consider it to be an accurate indicator.

current return on equity (ROE)   A ratio that measures profitability as the return on common stockholders' equity. It is calculated by dividing the reported earnings per share for the latest 12-month period by the book value per share.

current yield   This is a bond's annual interest payment as a percentage of its current market price. The current yield is calculated by dividing the annual coupon interest for a bond by the current market price. The coupon rate and the current yield on a bond are equal when the bond is selling at par. Thus, a $1,000 bond with a coupon of 10 percent that is currently selling at $1,000 will have a current yield of 10.0 percent. However, if the bond's price drops to $800, the current yield becomes 12.5 percent.

deferred annuity   This is an annuity whose contract provides that payments to the annuitant be postponed until a number of periods have elapsed, for example, when the annuitant attains a certain age.

disclosure statement Within a financial institution, this document should be signed by clients stating they understand the product they are buying is not insured by the FDIC, the value of the investment can and will fluctuate, they understand they will be charged a sales charge on securities, they have received and read the prospectus provided for their investment, and they understand the risks associated with the product they are buying.

disintermediation This is defined as the movement of funds from low-yielding accounts at traditional banking institutions to higher-yielding investments in the general market. Since banking deregulation, disintermediation is not the economic problem it once was.

diversification In broad terms, a bank client might diversify his or her investments among mutual funds, real estate, international investments, and money market instruments. A mutual fund might diversify by investing in many companies in many different industry groups. Diversification also can refer to the way large sponsors reduce risk by using multiple mutual fund styles.

Dow Jones Industrial Average (DJIA) A price-weighted average of 30 leading blue-chip industrial stocks, calculated by adding the prices of the 30 stocks and adjusting by a divisor, which reflects any stock dividends or splits. The Dow Jones Industrial Average is the most widely quoted index of the stock market, but it is not widely used as a benchmark for evaluating performance. The S&P 500 Index, which is more representative of the market, is the benchmark most widely used by performance measurement services.

duration The average life of the remaining cash flows from a bond or bond fund, including both interest and principal, weighted by the present value of each cash flow. It is determined by calculating the present value of each coupon and principal repayment, multiplying each result by the time before payment is to occur, dividing each result by the total present value, and summing.

EPS (earnings per share) growth This is the annualized rate of growth in reported earnings per share of stock.

equities Generally refers to common or preferred stocks. Claims of both common and preferred stockholders are junior to claims of bondholders or other creditors of the company. Holders of common stock assume the greater risk but generally exercise a greater degree of control and may gain the greater reward in the form of dividend growth and capital appreciation.

ERISA   The Employee Retirement Income Security Act of 1974. The stated purpose of ERISA is to protect the interests of workers who participate in private pension and welfare plans and their beneficiaries. The law governs how funds are administered and managed.

exchange privilege   This is a shareholder's right to switch from one mutual fund to another within one fund family. This is often done at no additional charge. This enables investors to put their money in an aggressive growth-stock fund, for example, when they expect the market to turn up strongly, then switch to a money market fund when they anticipate a downturn.

execution price   The negotiated price at which a security is purchased or sold.

fixed annuities   Guarantee the safety of the premium deposits. They also guarantee the initial interest rates for a specified time period. The guarantee is provided by the issuer (generally an insurance company) and never by the U.S. government or the Federal Reserve.

Four Great Lies   These are Time Series Lie, Account Selectivity Lie, Account Attrition Lie, and Replacement Lie. See **gullibility.**

frictional cash   Uninvested assets remaining after the purchase or sale of stocks or bonds, plus any dividends or interest recently received. These generally are deposited in money market funds until enough money is accumulated to purchase more stocks or bonds.

fundamentals   This word refers to the financial statistics that traditional analysts and many valuation models use. Fundamental data include stock, earnings, dividends, assets and liabilities, inventories, debt, and so on. Fundamental data are in contrast to items used in technical analysis—such as price momentum, volume trends, and short sales statistics.

gullibility   Buying scattered assets.

index fund   An index mutual fund is a passively managed portfolio designed and computer controlled to track the performance of a certain index, such as the S&P 500. In general, such mutual funds have performance within a few basis points of the target index. The most popular index mutual funds are those that track the S&P 500, but special index funds, such as those based on the Russell 1000 or the Wilshire 5000, are also available.

indicated dividends   For a single stock, the indicated dividend is typically the latest quarterly dividend multiplied by four.

intrinsic value   This means the theoretical valuation or price for a stock. The valuation is determined using a valuation theory or model. The resulting value is compared with the current market price. If the intrinsic value is greater than the market price, the stock is considered undervalued.

investment styles

- balanced—This term can be applied to any kind of portfolio that uses fixed income (bonds) as well as equity securities to reach goals. Many "boutique" investment managers are balanced managers, because it permits them to tailor the securities in a portfolio to the specific clients' cash flow needs and objectives.

- emerging growth—Here, a manager is looking for industries and companies whose growth rates are likely to be both rapid and independent of the overall stock market. "Emerging," of course, means new. This implies such companies may be relatively small in size with the potential to grow much larger. Such stocks are generally much more volatile than the stock market in general and require constant, close attention to developments.

- fixed-income—This term largely speaks for itself. Fixed-income fund managers invest money in bonds, notes, and other debt instruments. They have a broad range of styles, involving market timing, swapping to gain quality or yield, setting up maturity ladders, and so forth. A typical division of the fixed income market is between short (up to 3 years), intermediate (3 to 15 years), and long (15 to 30 years).

- income/growth—The primary purpose in security selection here is to achieve a current dividend yield significantly higher than the S&P 500. The stability of the dividend and the rate of growth of the dividend are also of concern to the income buyer. These portfolios may own more utilities, may be less high tech, and may own convertible preferreds and convertible bonds.

■ money market fund—money market fund managers invest in short-term fixed instruments and cash equivalents. These instruments make up the portfolio and their objective is to maximize principal protection. Even though these accounts have short-term (one-day) liquidity, they typically pay more like 90- to 180-day CDs versus passbook or one-week CDs.

■ quality growth—This term implies long-term investment in high quality growth stocks, some of which might be larger, emerging companies while others might be long-established household names. Such a portfolio might have volatility equal to or above that of the overall market, but less than that of an "emerging growth" portfolio.

■ value—In this instance, the manager uses various tests to determine an intrinsic value for a given security, and tries to purchase the security substantially below that value. The goal and hope are that the stock price in the fund will ultimately rise to the stock's fair value or above. Price to earnings, price to sales, price to cash flow, price to book value, and price to break-up value (or true net asset value) are some of the ratios examined in such an approach.

load funds A mutual fund that is sold for a sales charge (load) by a brokerage firm or other sales representative. Such funds may be stock, bond, or commodity funds, with conservative or aggressive objectives. The stated advantage of a load fund is that the salesperson will explain the fund to the client and advise him or her when it is appropriate to sell as well as when to buy more shares. See **churning.**

lump-sum distribution Single payment to a beneficiary covering the entire amount of an agreement. Participants in Individual Retirement Accounts, pension plans, profit-sharing, and executive stock option plans generally can opt for a lump-sum distribution if the taxes are not too burdensome when they become eligible.

management fee (mutual fund)   Charge against investor assets for managing the portfolio of an open- or closed-end mutual fund as well as for such services as shareholder relations or administration. The fee, as disclosed in the prospectus, is a fixed percentage of the fund's asset value, typically 1 percent or less per year.

market bottom   The date the Bear leg of the market cycle reaches its low, not identified until some time after the fact. Market bottoms also can be defined as the month-end or quarter-end closest to the actual bottom date. It's also the date that most individual investors throw in the towel by selling out and the date that most stockbrokers quit to become mortgage loans sales agents.

market capitalization   The current value of a company determined by multiplying the latest available number of outstanding common shares by the current market price of a share. Market cap is also an indication of the trading liquidity of a particular issue.

market cycle   A period of falling prices followed by a period of rising prices, or vice versa. Cycles are measured peak-to-peak or trough-to-trough. The rising leg (called the Bull Market) and the falling leg (the Bear Market) make a complete market cycle. The major performance measuring services, such as SEI, do not measure from a precise peak to a precise bottom, but use the nearest complete calendar quarter. The start or end of a market cycle is not known until after the fact.

market peak   The date the Bull leg of the market cycle reaches its high, not confirmed until some time after the fact. Market peaks also can be defined as the month-end or quarter-end closest to the actual peak date. It also is the date that individual investors cash out CDs at a penalty and jump into the market. It's also when mortgage sales agents become stock brokers, and 50 new mutual funds are opened by wire house firms.

market timing   This is defined as the attempt to base investment decisions on the expected direction of the market. If stocks are expected to decline, the timer may elect to hold a portion of the portfolio in cash equivalents or bonds. Timers may base their decisions on fundamentals (e.g., selling stocks when the market's price/book ratio reaches a certain level), on technical considerations (such as declining momentum or excessive investor optimism), or a combination of both. No one has a sustained record as a successful market timer except at cocktail parties.

market value   Is the market or liquidation value of a given security or of an entire pool of assets.

mutual fund families   A mutual fund sponsor or company usually offers a number of funds with different investment objectives within its family of funds. For example, a mutual fund family may include a money market fund, a government bond fund, a corporate bond fund, a blue chip stock fund, and a more speculative stock fund. If an investor buys a fund in the family, he or she is allowed to exchange that fund for another in the same family. This is usually done with no additional sales charge.

National Association of Securities Dealers, Inc. (NASD)
The principal association of over-the-counter (OTC) brokers and dealers that establishes legal and ethical standards of conduct for its members. NASD was established in 1939 to regulate the OTC market in much the same manner as organized exchanges monitor actions of their members.

net asset value (NAV)   This is defined as the market value of each share of a mutual fund. This figure is derived by taking a fund's total assets (securities, cash, and receivables), deducting liabilities, and then dividing that total by the number of shares outstanding. In other words, it is after marketing, distribution, and 3-color brochure expenses.

net trade   Generally, this is an over-the-counter trade involving no explicit commission. The representative's compensation is in the spread between the cost of the security and the price paid by the client. Also, it is a trade in which shares are exchanged directly with the issuer. This practice is under intense scrutiny by the SEC and may eventually be revealed as illegal, immoral, and unethical, and maybe not.

no-load funds   Mutual fund offered by an open-end investment company that imposes no sales charge (load) on its shareholders. Investors buy shares in no-load funds directly from the fund companies, rather than through a broker, as is done in load funds. Because no broker is used, no advice is given on when to buy or sell.

nominal return   This is the actual current dollar growth in an asset's value over a given period. See also **total return** and **real return.**

open-end fund   A mutual fund is considered "open-end" if it regularly sells an unlimited number of shares directly to shareholders and buys them back at NAV whenever shareholders wish to redeem or sell them.

packaged products   Specific types of products underwritten and packaged by manufacturing companies that can be bought and sold directly through those companies. Packaged products are not required to go through a clearing process. Packaged products include mutual funds, unit investment trusts (UIT), limited partnership interests, and annuities. See **conflict of interest.**

passive manager   A manager who purchases bonds for a trust. He does little or no trading after purchasing the initial portfolio.

percentage points   Used to describe the difference between two readings that are percentages. For example, if a portfolio's performance was 18.2 percent versus the S&P 500's 14.65, it outperformed the S&P by 3.6 percentage points. See **basis point** to talk the lingo.

portfolio   A portfolio is the combined holdings of more than one stock, bond, commodity, real estate investment, cash equivalent, or other asset by an individual or institutional investor. The purpose of a portfolio is to reduce risk by diversification. See **scattered assets.**

price/earnings (P/E) ratio   This may be defined as the current price divided by reported earnings per share of stock for the latest 12-month period. For example, a stock with earnings per share during the trailing year of $5 and currently selling at $50 per share has a price/earnings ratio of 10.

product vendor   A firm, such as an insurance or mutual fund company, that manufactures securities or insurance products, maintains selling agreements with third-party firms to distribute those products to subscribers, and provides marketing support materials. Most third-party marketing firms offer products that are manufactured by product vendors. See **scattered assets.**

proprietary fund   A mutual fund or fund family that is manufactured by the bank, third-party firm, or company with which it is affiliated. See **scattered assets.**

proxy   This is a form or ballot permitting a shareholder to vote on corporate matters.

quartile Is a ranking of comparative portfolio performance. The top 25 percent of mutual fund managers are in the 1st Quartile, those ranking from 26 percent to 50 percent are in the 2nd Quartile, from 51 percent to 75 percent in the 3rd Quartile, and the lowest 25 percent in the 4th Quartile. You should seek 1st Quartile and be satisfied with 2nd.

rank This word refers to a percentile performance ranking with the 1st percentile being the highest and 99th being the lowest. The ranking evaluates a manager's performance in relation to other managers. For example, a 10th percentile ranking means that this mutual fund manager has performed better than 90 percent of mutual fund managers in the comparative universe for similar funds.

real return This is the inflation-adjusted return on an asset. Inflation-adjusted returns are calculated by subtracting the rate of inflation from an asset's apparent, or nominal, return. For example, if common stocks earn a total return of 10.3 percent over a period of time, but inflation during that period is 3.1 percent, the real return is the difference: 7.2 percent. Between 1926 and 1995, the real and nominal returns on selected financial assets were as follows:

Asset Class	Nominal Return	Real Return
Common stocks	10.3%	7.2%
Long-term bonds		
Corporate	5.2%	2.1%
Government	4.6%	1.5%
Treasury bills	3.6%	0.5%

registered investment advisor (RIA) A firm or individual that provides investment management services for a fee and is under the regulatory authority of the Securities and Exchange Commission (SEC).

reinvested dividends It refers to dividends paid by a particular mutual fund that are reinvested in that same mutual fund. Some bank funds offer automatic dividend reinvestment programs. In the complex equation theoretically used to determine the performance of the S&P 500, each company's dividend is reinvested in the stock of that company.

relative return The return of a stock or a mutual fund portfolio compared with some index, usually the S&P 500.

risk   Investment risk is the actual variability or expected uncertainty of investment returns over a given period of time. This variability or uncertainty causes "rational" investors to expect higher returns on investments where the actual timing or amount of payoffs is not guaranteed. A bank mutual fund portfolio has two types of risk. The first, called market risk, captures the amount of portfolio variability caused by events that have an impact on the market as a whole. The second risk is gullibility.

risk-free rate of return   The return on an asset that is considered virtually riskless. U.S. government Treasury bills are typically used as the risk-free asset because of their short time horizon and the low probability of default.

S&P 500   The performance benchmark most widely used by sponsors, managers, and performance measurement services. This index includes 400 industrial stocks, 20 transportation stocks, 40 financial stocks, and 40 public utilities. Performance is measured on a capitalization-weighted basis. The index is maintained by Standard & Poor's Corporation, a subsidiary of McGraw-Hill Inc.

S&P common stock rankings   The S&P rankings measure historical growth and stability of earnings and dividends. The system includes nine rankings:

A+, A, A–	Above average
B+	Average
B, B–, C	Below average
NR	Insufficient historical data or not amenable to the ranking process. As a matter of policy, S&P does not rank the stocks of foreign companies, investment companies, and certain finance-oriented companies.
D	Company is in reorganization—The soup

The S&P ranking does not reflect all factors relating to a stock's quality because it does not consider a company's balance sheet or financial resources.

scattered assets   A collection of assets that were sold as good ideas at the time; now you own them and don't know why.

Securities Act of 1933 and Securities Exchange of 1934   The keystone laws in the regulation of securities markets. These govern exchanges, over-the-counter markets, broker-dealers, the conduct of secondary markets, extension of credit in securities transactions, the conduct of corporate insiders, and principally the prohibition of fraud and manipulation in securities transactions. They also outline the powers of the Securities and Exchange Commission (SEC) to interpret, supervise, and enforce the securities laws of the United States. (They have a badge, a gun, and handcuffs—don't break the rules.)

securities investor protection corporation (SIPC)   This is a government-sponsored organization created in 1970 to insure investor accounts at brokerage firms in the event of the brokerage firm's insolvency and liquidation. The maximum insurance of $500,000, including a maximum of $100,000 in cash assets per account, covers client losses due to brokerage house insolvency, not client losses caused by security price fluctuations. SIPC coverage is conceptually similar to Federal Deposit Insurance Corporation coverage of client accounts at commercial banks.

standard deviation   This is a statistical measure of the variation or dispersion of a sample from the average of the sample. The sample can be one of price moves, total returns, or other groups of observations. The standard deviation is calculated as follows:

$$\text{Standard Deviation} = \frac{\sum_{i-1}^{n}\left(x_i - x\right)^2}{n-1}$$

The expression within the square root is essentially the average of the squared deviations of each observation from the average of the total sample. The deviations are squared to eliminate the effects of negative differences. As a rule, approximately two-thirds of the sample fall within one standard deviation (plus or minus) around the average of the sample, and 95 percent of the observations will fall within two standard deviations.

One example of how standard deviation might be used as an indicator of risk is found in Ibbotson Associates' Stocks, Bonds, Bills, and Inflation Database as of December 29, 1989. Market results for the years 1926 through 1989 show the following annualized returns and standard deviations:

	Annualized Returns	Standard Deviation
Small stocks	12.3%	35.1%
Common stocks	10.3	20.7
Long-term corporate bonds	5.2	8.4
Long-term government bonds	4.6	8.5
U.S. Treasury bills	3.6	3.3

In most cases, the higher the return, the higher the standard deviation. This underscores the fact that, in general, higher returns are accompanied by higher risk.

stock broker   A sales agent working for a commission.

strategic asset allocation   Determines an appropriate asset mix for a client based on long-term capital market conditions, expected returns, and risks.

systemic withdrawal plan   A program in which shareholders receive payments from their mutual fund investments at regular intervals. Typically, these payments are drawn first from the fund's dividends and capital gains distribution, if any, and then from principal as needed.

12b-1 Mutual Fund   Mutual fund that assesses shareholders for some of its "promotion" expenses. These funds are usually no-load, so no brokers are involved in the sale to the public. Instead, the funds normally rely on advertising and public relations to build their assets. The charge usually amounts to about 1 percent or less of a fund's assets. A 12b-1 fund must be specifically registered as such with the Securities and Exchange Commission, and the fact that such charges are levied must be disclosed. See **Four Great Lies.**

T-bills   Are promissory notes issued by the U.S. Treasury and sold through competitive bidding, with a short-term maturity date, usually 13 to 26 weeks. The return on T-bills has almost no variation, so it serves as a proxy for a "riskless" investment.

technical analysis   Any investment approach that judges the attractiveness of particular stocks or the market as a whole based on market data, such as price patterns, volume, momentum, or investor sentiment, as opposed to fundamental financial data, such as earnings dividends.

time weighted rate of return   The rate at which a dollar invested at the beginning of a period would grow if no additional capital were invested and no cash withdrawals were made. It provides an indication of value added by the investment manager, and allows comparisons to the performance of other investment managers and market indexes.

total return   A standard measure of performance or return including both capital appreciation (or depreciation) and dividends or other income received. For example, Stock A is priced at $60 at the start of a year and pays an annual dividend of $4. If the stock moves up to $70 in price, the appreciation component is 16.7 percent, the yield component is 6.7 percent, and the total return is 23.4 percent. That oversimplification does not take into account any earnings on the reinvested dividends.

transaction costs Another term for execution costs or commissions. Total transaction costs (or the cost of buying and selling stocks) have three components: (1) the actual dollars paid in commissions, (2) the market impact—that is, the impact a manager's trade has on the market price for the stock (this varies with the size of the trade and the skill of the trader), and (3) the opportunity cost of the return (positive or negative) given up by not executing the trade instantaneously.

turnover Turnover is the volume or percentage of buying or selling activity within a mutual fund portfolio relative to the mutual fund portfolio's size.

up and down market analysis This is a measure of the manager's performance in both up and down markets relative to the market itself. An "up" value of 110 suggests the manager performs 10 percent better than the market when the market is up. A "down" value of 90 suggests the manager's loss is only nine-tenths of the market's loss.

During the selected time period, the quarterly market return is considered a down market if it is less than zero. It is an up market if it is greater than or equal to zero. The Down Market Capture Ratio is calculated by dividing the manager's return during the down market quarters by the market's return during the same quarters. The Up Market Capture Ratio is calculated by dividing the manager's return during up market quarters by the market's return during the same quarters.

Ideally, the manager will have a ratio greater than 100 in the up markets, showing that they outperformed when the market was rising, and less than 100 in the down markets, showing relative capital preservation in weak markets.

value added These are returns over and above those of the stock market or relative index.

variable annuities   Insurance-based investment products, which like other forms of annuities allow for growth of invested premiums to be free from taxation until withdrawals are made from the contract. Unique to variable annuities are several forms of investment alternatives that vary in both its potential for reward and risk. Variable annuity choices are broad enough that an investor can employ either an aggressive or conservative approach, or a combination of both, while enjoying the benefits of tax-deferred growth. Guarantee of principal from loss upon death of the owner is covered by a death benefit provision.

volatility   The extent to which market values and investment returns are uncertain or fluctuate. Another word for risk, volatility is gauged using such measures as beta, mean absolute deviation, and standard deviation.

wrap fee   A fee that bundles the services that includes consulting services, custodianship of assets, and brokerage transactions. This fee is sometimes known as an all-inclusive fee.

yield (current yield)   For stocks, yield is the percentage return paid in dividends on a common or preferred stock, calculated by dividing the indicated annual dividend by the market price of the stock. For example, if a stock sells for $40 and pays a dividend of $2 per share, it has a yield of 5 percent (i.e., $2 divided by $40).

For bonds, the coupon rate of interest divided by the market price is called current yield. For example, a bond selling for $1,000 with a 10 percent coupon offers a 10 percent current yield. If the same bond were selling for $500, it would offer a 20 percent yield to an investor who bought it for $500. (As a bond's price falls, its yield rises, and vice versa.)

yield to maturity   The discount rate that equates the present value of the bond's cash flows (semi-annual coupon payments, the redemption value) with the market price. The yield to maturity will actually be earned if (1) the investor holds the bond to maturity and (2) the investor is able to reinvest all coupon payments at a rate equal to the yield to maturity. When a bond is selling at par, the yield to maturity and the coupon rate are equal.

INDEX